Santa Fe 1880

Santa Fe 1880

―――――――――◆―――――――――

Chronicles from the Year of the Railroad

Allen R. Steele

Published by The History Press
Charleston, SC
www.historypress.com

Copyright © 2019 by Allen R. Steele
All rights reserved

Front cover, top: Photograph by J.R. Riddle; courtesy of the Palace of the Governors Photo Archives (NMHM/DCA) negative 076033.
Front cover, bottom: Courtesy of the New Mexico Capitol Art Foundation.
Back cover: Photograph by Ben Wittick; courtesy of the Palace of the Governors Photo Archives (NMHM/DCA) negative 015780.

First published 2019

Manufactured in the United States

ISBN 9781467141949

Library of Congress Control Number: 2018966271

Notice: The information in this book is true and complete to the best of our knowledge. It is offered without guarantee on the part of the author or The History Press. The author and The History Press disclaim all liability in connection with the use of this book.

All rights reserved. No part of this book may be reproduced or transmitted in any form whatsoever without prior written permission from the publisher except in the case of brief quotations embodied in critical articles and reviews.

Contents

Forewords, by Andrew Lovato, PhD, and Ana Pacheco   7
Acknowledgements   9
Introduction   11

1. Winter of Discontent   17
2. Frontier Politics   24
3. A Trade School for Girls   33
4. Chasing Vitorio   41
5. Santa Fe's Triumph   47
6. Boom Times   54
7. Train Heaven   61
8. The Archbishop Recovers   68
9. The Governor Writes a Book   74
10. The Stolen Madonna   79
11. Closing in on Vitorio   87
12. A Flooded Desert   92
13. The Governor at Wit's End   99
14. The Lamy Murder Trial   107
15. Mexico's Hero   112
16. A Presidential Visit   118
17. A Tale of the Christ   125
18. Winter Returns   131
19. The Kid Comes Back to Santa Fe   140
20. Varied Destinies   147

Selected Bibliography   155
About the Author   159

Forewords

The year 1880 was a watershed one in the evolution of the small town that sat at the foot of the Sangre de Cristo Mountains. Santa Fe was used to change, and its long history reflected this. Beginning as early as the thirteenth and fourteen centuries, when several large native settlements were established along the Santa Fe River and then abandoned, cultural and territorial shifts swept the region.

In 1607, Juan de Oñate established the village of Santa Fe as the capital of Spain's northern outpost in the New World. In 1680, the Pueblo Revolt drove the Spanish from Santa Fe, and Pueblo Indians occupied the city until Don Diego de Vargas reclaimed it in 1693. In 1846, American troops occupied Santa Fe during the Mexican-American War, which led to Santa Fe being declared a territory of the United States in 1850. In 1862, the Confederate flag flew over Santa Fe for a brief period before Union soldiers reoccupied the city.

Thus by 1880, the people of Santa Fe were already hardened to change and veterans of the unpredictable tides of history. However, even by these standards, the future would bring a bewildering wave of transformation. The coming of the railroad bringing new settlers from the East, the changing role of the church and the struggle to maintain law and order were some of the challenges and opportunities facing the citizenry of Santa Fe.

In this book, Allen Steele captures these exuberant and turbulent times by examining Santa Fe through the lens of one year in which the character and future of Santa Fe would be forever altered. Steele uses the voices of several

Forewords

Santa Fe characters during this period to describe the mood of the times using a narrative style that brings to life the events and changes taking place. It is in the details described by the voices of Susan Wallace, Sister Blandina and others that the true picture of Santa Fe in 1880 emerges.

Steele tells a story of hardship, corruption and greed that is integrated with the opposite qualities of generosity, compassion and joy that paints an honest picture of the experience of living in Santa Fe during this period. This book suggests that history does not necessarily need to be presented as a dry recitation of dates and facts but is more enjoyable and palatable when told through the thoughts and emotions of those who were impacted by the times.

Perhaps, history is less about great events and dates than it is about the lives of people and what they had to do to thrive and endure.

—Andrew Lovato, PhD
Santa Fe City Historian

It was 1880 and the railroad had come to Santa Fe! The arrival of people from afar, who were bound together in their hopes and dreams, forever defining the landscape of New Mexico's state capital. This confluence of diversity brought social change through foresight, determination, fame and infamy. The Frenchman, Archbishop Jean-Baptiste Lamy, re-created a Romanesque monument to his country with the Cathedral Basilica of St. Francis of Assisi in the heart of downtown Santa Fe. The Italian nun, Sister Blandina, nurtured to the poor and suffering, bargaining with fate at every corner. Adolf Bandelier of Switzerland set out to study an ancient civilization providing a blueprint of the past. Governor Lew Wallace wrote the epic *Ben-Hur* that became the greatest Christian novel of the 19th century. Chief Vitorio was the Apache warrior who resisted the headwinds of change creating havoc for all intent on altering the landscape. And the lawlessness of the West reached new heights through the antics of Billy the Kid. Like each railroad track, these people were linked to the future of Santa Fe.

—Ana Pacheco, Historian and Author

Acknowledgements

My sincere appreciation goes to all the individuals and institutions that gave so generously of their time and knowledge. Without their help, these revelations of Santa Fe's past, and especially the incredible year of 1880, may not have been recorded. The patient attention of the librarians at the New Mexico State Library was exceptional. The expert and prompt assistance of employees at the Palace of the Governors was most helpful. Among those who gave encouragement and support were

Andrea Steele
Robert Felix
Ana Pacheco
Ann Hillerman
Andrew Lovato
Ed Pulsifer
Peter Sinclair
Andrew Brawner
Elsie and Larry Davis
Rick Blythe
Sita Jamieson-Caddle
Raúl Burciaga
Mimi Stewart

Introduction

Santa Fe…is a wretched collection of mud-houses…the appearance of the town defies description, and I can compare it to nothing but a dilapidated brick-kiln or a prairie-dog town. The inhabitants are worthy of their city, and a more miserable, vicious-looking population it would be impossible to imagine," wrote George Frederick Augustus Ruxton in 1846. His travel adventures took him from Vera Cruz on the Mexican coast, through the heart of Mexico, up the Rio Grande and north to the Rocky Mountains.

The Englishman did not stay long in the city. "Although I determined to remain some time in Santa Fe…I was so disgusted with the filth of the town, and the disreputable society a stranger was forced into, that in a very few days I once more packed my mules, and proceeded to the north."

Later that same year, another visitor, an American woman, recorded her impressions of the city. Susan Magoffin, wife of an American trader, arrived after a long trek on the Santa Fe Trail "at such a late hour it was rather difficult for me to form any idea of the city." In her diary she remembered walking down a long hill into the main street, "which as in any other city has squares; but I must say they are singularly occupied. One Square may be a dwelling-house, a church or something of the kind, and immediately opposite to it occupying the whole square is a cornfield."

She was pleased to find a river running through it, "affording me a fair opportunity to enjoy that luxury to the fullest extent." It served as her source for drinking and bathing water as it did everyone else in town. A church,

Introduction

located at the western end of the main street was "well supplied with bells, which are chiming, it seems to me, all the time both night and day."

One of the first American women to travel the trail from Missouri to the New Mexico capital, Susan Magoffin was herself a new attraction in the remote city, especially for the recently arrived U.S. Army men under the command of General Stephen Watts Kearny. The recent outcome of the Mexican-American War was considered a done deal, and the Army was sent to secure the territory, indeed the whole Southwest, for the United States.

A building called the Palace of the Governors dominated a whole side of the city's central square. The seat of government since 1610, the adobe building stretched along the north side of the plaza about three hundred feet. With walls three feet thick and a long porch running the full length, it stood one-story high. Thanks to the newly arrived Army, a flagpole now stood in the middle of the city plaza with an American flag wafting at its top.

And that is just how a Confederate army found the city when it invaded in the spring of 1862. It was Civil War! In an attempt to take over the Union territory of New Mexico and push north to Denver and march on to California, an Army from Texas arrived in Santa Fe on March 16. They found the city silent and smoky. The U.S. Army quartermaster, warned of their advance on the capital, ordered all military supplies in the city burned. Military and governmental headquarters relocated to Las Vegas, New Mexico, sixty miles east. Soon the Confederate flag flew atop a pole in the plaza.

It flew there for nearly two weeks. When the Confederates flooded the capital in retreat from their loss at nearby Glorieta Pass, local citizens calmly watched for an opportunity to pull the strange flag down. They raised the familiar Stars and Stripes. Within days, the easy ways of the old city returned.

Some forty years later, in 1878, a new governor, General Lew Wallace, arrived in Santa Fe with orders from the president to clean up the wild west territory. As a government official, he provided descriptions of the city that are also rather colorless. But not so those of his wife, Susan, whose writings reveal the heart and soul of the sleepy city. Writing to entertain readers back East, she found the dusty capital a subject of her sophisticated disdain. To her, the simple lifestyle and ancient traditions were a source of curiosity and entertainment.

Nevertheless, her descriptions of the capital city, established well over 250 years before she arrived, give credible insight into the daily life of one of America's earliest municipalities. Founded by the Spanish, it eventually became a Mexican territorial capital when that country expelled the Spanish in 1821, creating a new republic. Mexico, in turn, lost its northern territory

Introduction

when the United States won the Mexican-American War, culminating with the Treaty of Guadalupe Hidalgo. That treaty turned over to the Americans all the vast lands between Texas and the Pacific Ocean.

During centuries of history, a variety of people of different cultures crisscrossed New Mexico's dry deserts, prairies and mountains long before the Wallaces arrived. In the process, the Spanish, the Mexicans and the Americans violated the ancient lands of the Native Americans in turn, and by 1879, the enchanted territory was a melting pot of cultures and people, much like its latest conqueror, the United States. The Wallaces saw the old capital city with new eyes.

Susan Wallace found the city dirty and unkempt, swarming with hungry dogs. The most common sound heard in the streets was the braying of burros, the main beast of burden among the citizens. At the western edge of the city was Burro Alley, the stabling place for the pack trains that arrived periodically bringing food and goods by vendors from as far away as Mexico City, along the Camino Real. Chopped wood, an important commodity for keeping the fireplaces going, was brought to town on the backs of burros. Susan even referred to a "Burro Cavalry" stationed at the Army garrison!

She observed that vagrants congregated in the plaza in the middle of town. She admired the handsome Pueblo Indians whom she saw in the city streets: "Fine fellows, clad in white with hair tressed behind and hanging down on each side." No doubt from time to time she stopped on a rutted street to chat with the owners of mercantile stores or their wives, many of Jewish origin. And the priestly robes of padres were a common sight along the dusty streets.

But among the strange and dusty anomalies of life in the town, aspects of civilization were evident. She found it had "the charm of foreign flavor, and like San Antonio, retains some portion of the grace which long lingers about, if indeed it ever forsakes, the spot where Spain has held rule for centuries." Furthermore, newly arriving citizens could have a pleasant evening at singing parties held in the evenings at the First National Bank. The Union Restaurant advertised meals available at all hours for thirty-five cents, and at Miller's Summer Garden people enjoyed refreshing drinks, and they rolled ten pins. Miller's also offered fresh Baltimore oysters with the meal.

On the other hand, Susan Wallace was often mindful of the wildness of the high desert and nearby mountains, where bear, mountain lions, deer, elk, wolves and coyotes roamed in abundance. One evening as she walked with her husband, they came upon a grisly sight: a coyote was tearing a stray lamb to pieces, within sight of the girls' school chapel. The animal glared at them for a moment then quietly and leisurely stalked away.

A special feature of the town was the Santa Fe River, the real source of life for the capital. Snowmelt mixed with natural springs brought cold, clear water to the city, but a water distribution system had yet to be established. In a regular scene, apparently a Tuesday event by tradition, local women gathered on the river's sandy banks to make a little fire for washing clothes. "Her machine is one bucket and a square tin box. She pounds the clothes between two stones…She boils them in the box set on granite, rinses in the pure snow-water and spreads them on the rocks to dry," Susan wrote.

On another occasion, Susan and Lew Wallace went to visit a local family who lived in a neighborhood just outside the main city perimeter. Crossing a sandy arroyo, a dry creek bed, then stumbling along a stony path, they suddenly came up against a wall. "It is about six feet high, made of mud mixed with ashes, coal, cow horns, hoofs, mule bones, barrel hoops, the wheels of a baby wagon, cans, broken bottles, boots, curry-combs," she wrote.

The top of the wall bristled with scraps of tin, embedded in the adobe wall to discourage invaders from jumping over it. The entrance gate, made of dwarf cedar logs, was bound together by rawhide strings. Its wooden hinges groaned and creaked as they opened it, designed to alert the residents of anyone approaching.

Once in the courtyard, they found the owner and his wife "in the artistic pose called squat, at leisure profound, if not elegant." Inside was the earthen floor swept clean with branches of Spanish broom; the makeshift broom was left leaning against the mud fireplace in the corner. "There were no andirons, shovel or tongs, and when fire is made the wood is placed on end against the back of the fireplace. Chests, a few pieces of crockery on a pine table, complete the furniture."

In contrast, her husband's office was located in the Palace of the Governors. To the building's north, she noticed an open field that contained neither grass, weeds nor moss, "not even a straggling sage-bush or forlorn cactus; nothing but bare desert sand and a solitary cottonwood tree. On two sides of the vacant lot were high adobe walls, on the third side were government buildings and on the fourth side, partly abandoned office buildings."

As she wandered about the place, her curiosity became acute; she decided to do some investigating. She found a key to the rooms and went exploring. At the first door, she fitted the key into the rough, old-fashioned lock and "pushing with all my strength, it slowly swung on rusty hinges, into a room, perhaps seventeen by twenty feet in size, barely high enough for a man to stand upright in." Mice scattered about at her intrusion, and a musty smell filled her nostrils. As her eyes became adjusted to the darkness, she realized she had entered the historic records room of New Mexico.

In barrels and boxes and on piles on the floor lay the records of nearly three hundred years. She found items from 1580 up to 1879. Old weather-stained official documents, letters, copies of reports and dispatches marked the ages of political change. Without the dry desert air of New Mexico, many of the items would have mildewed into nothing long before. She went to work organizing the records of centuries.

She was also intrigued by reports of turquoise mines south of the city that anciently supplied the Indian markets of the Americas. "It (turquoise) is valued by the Navajo beyond the garnets and beryls of his own country," she said in her admiration of the precious gems. She noted it was used as currency among the Pueblos. "The Indian girls along the Colorado wear it as a love-token in their necklaces; the roving and tameless Apache covets a blue bead as an amulet; the degraded Ute loves its soft glimmer; and when a Mohave chief would assume regal splendor, he sticks a three-cornered piece of chalcocite (turquoise) into his royal nose!"

Not many miles to the south were the famous mines of the Placer, Sandia, and Manzana Mountains. In these ranges were located three main turquoise mines. She decided to make an excursion to the town of Cerrillos one summer day where "these blue-eyed gems are found, the only mines as yet discovered this side of the Russian seas!" She packed a lunch and hired a wagon and driver to take her and a couple lady friends on the outing.

As they set out for the mines under clear blue skies, Susan Wallace noted the "Gama grass, low and dry, the cactus the only shrub in sight." She watched prairie dogs scatter as the wagon approached, each colony warned by its watchful sentinels. As the noon hour approached, the stillness of the countryside was unnerving. "The sun came up with a dry, sultry scorch, like flame. Our spirits flagged."

When they finally reached the largest mine, they discovered it was "half a mountain cut away…the yawning pit is two hundred feet deep and more than three hundred in diameter!" Crushed rock and chips lying all around gave evidence of centuries of toil by men of different worlds searching for gems to bring them or their masters riches untold. "Resting in the fragrant shade of the pines, we talked of Montezuma, the saddest, proudest chief of Indian history, whose name is still a majestic memory among the…Pueblos."

On their circuitous return to Santa Fe they "passed the white tents of the vanguard of civilization—an army of laborers, working day and night on the railroad track." On reflecting on the scene, she made her own prediction, "The waste lands of the wandering tribes will be divided and sold by the acre…the Mexican will be jostled on the elbow, and will wake from his long trance to find himself in the way."

Her prolific writings about her experiences in this remote land indicate an uncomfortable sojourn: they are the words of a curious observer, not someone who came to stay. Her correspondence shows deep devotion to her husband and a pride in his appointment as governor. But it could not overcome her feeling of being a stranger in a strange land. Perhaps a threat by Billy the Kid was the final straw: "I mean to ride into the Plaza at Santa Fe, hitch my horse in front of the Palace, and put a bullet through Lew Wallace."

In late 1879, she escaped the high desert and returned to her family home in Indiana. She would not be on hand to witness the great changes coming to the city or experience the incredible events that would challenge her husband in the new year of 1880. He was about to endure one of his most momentous years, without her at his side. She would only hear about it from a distance, through his letters.

1
Winter of Discontent

There is nothing better than for religion to support patriotism: and nothing wiser than for both to uphold and encourage domestic economy.
—*Mark Twain, quoted in the* Santa Fe New Mexican, *November 10, 1879*

The year 1880 did not start well for Jean-Baptiste Lamy, archbishop of New Mexico. He was flat on his back in bed with a high fever. And, like so many other people who get sick, he was quite cantankerous. In his anxiety at being sick, he was impatient and curt with those who tried to care for him. Even so, the Sisters of Loretto watched over him day and night. From an adjacent room, they listened for his slightest groan or call; they could respond at a moment's notice. For five days, he was close to death, so seriously that last sacraments were administered.

At first, only his niece Mary was his constant companion. One of the Sisters of Loretto, she was among those who taught at the girls' school the archbishop founded some years before. During the most trying time, she stayed with him around the clock for those critical five days. Although she had taken the name Sister Mary Francesca when she entered the Sisterhood, whenever he awoke to find her at his bedside, he affectionately called her by her French given name, Marie. But abruptly at a lucid moment in his delirium, he ordered her to leave him and send another Sister to take her place.

It was not only physical illness that caused his anguish: mentally, he was not ready to die. He had not completed his work. And a recent family

Santa Fe 1880

tragedy weighed heavily on his mind. He yearned to live so he could protect the vulnerable people of the diocese: the stalwart but poor Spanish and Mexican people who were eking out a living from the hard earth of the desert and the Native Americans who for centuries somehow coaxed corn, beans and squash to grow in the Rio Grande Valley for a subsistence living. His responsibilities and his love embraced them all. And he also cherished new friends in the old city of Santa Fe. The newly arrived Europeans and Americans were in the minority and because of it they became the best of friends, bound together by their isolation and sense of community building. He had to live—too much to do!

His major concern was for the spirituality of the Mexican population for whom he foresaw a sad future. "Very few of them will be able to follow modern progress," he wrote. "Seeing themselves on the one hand under American discipline and, on the other, imagining that the Americans prefer foreigners to them, their faith, which is still lively enough, would grow gradually weaker; and the consequences would be dreadful." He feared the clash of cultures and the collapse of the spiritual codes he had worked so hard to establish.

The better life he planned for all of them had yet to come. Yes, there was progress. His school for boys, and another for girls, functioned rather well. The little hospital that he created by giving up his residence for the cause was a lifesaver for those who needed its services. And the cathedral, his citadel for God in the city, was still under construction. Yet he faced the new year with a sense of foreboding because of the uncertainties he knew it would bring. He was not the only one trying to cope with the fog of the future. The whole city was coming to terms with uncertainty. But this holiday season, when they expected to see him visiting around the city as usual, everyone in town was alarmed at the archbishop's absence from the festivities.

Winter in northern New Mexico can be difficult. Nights can be very cold, even reaching single-digit temperatures. Snowfall is common, but sunny days quickly melt the white stuff, at least on southern exposures. Santa Fe, at 7,000 feet, can be penetratingly cold when the winds blow, especially for farmers, ranchers, miners and others who work outdoors. In 1880, the only source of human comfort on cold nights at home was the kiva fireplace in the corner of the room, stacked with pine logs teepee style.

The local newspaper, the *Santa Fe New Mexican*, for the first week of January was full of exciting news for the new year. The Atchison, Topeka & Santa Fe (AT&SF) Railway company was laying tracks westward at the rate of two miles per day, and the tracks, the editor predicted, should arrive in the city in just a few weeks. At the same time, engineers from the Denver & Rio Grande were in town surveying and locating lines for a planned rail entrance from the north.

The newspaper reported that Governor Lew Wallace had just returned from his own evaluation of the Indian threat to New Mexican towns in the south. He reported that Apache chief Vitorio and his band escaped into Mexico for the time being, but he expected the renegades to soon return to menace the territory. He would give a full report to the territorial legislature in session later that month.

Meanwhile, the niceties of social life, such as they were in the capital city in 1880, continued. The Christmas Bazaar was coming to a close at the J.L. Johnson halls on the east side of the central plaza. The decorative evergreen boughs were starting to droop, but the streamers, flags and Chinese lanterns still held their color.

The recent Christmas was still on everyone's mind when Major Baird, from the military post at Fort Marcy on the north side of town, arrived as Santa Claus to hand out tin whistles, toy railroads and horses and rattles to the children. Young Solomon Luna, a student at Santa Fe Academy, won a sofa pillow for being the most popular young man of the year.

A moment of excitement interrupted the holiday festivities when all the able men in town were called out to form a fire bucket brigade. The roof of Judge Prince's house was on fire. Located just off the main plaza in the heart of town, the historic structure was only slightly damaged thanks to early discovery of the fire and plenty of water in nearby horse troughs.

Thirty members of the Santa Fe Literary Club met the previous week to hear General John Smith read *The Burial of Sir John Moore* and *The Dying Christian*. It was announced that a guidebook to New Mexico was soon to be published.

The newspaper noted an influx of strangers on the streets and in the hotels. The three hotels, the Exchange, Herlow's and Miller's, were overrun with newcomers. More hotels were needed, yelled the editor! Rowdy bunches of people filled city saloons. A railroad employee by the name of John Diamond had just been shot and killed at the Texas Dance Hall by gambler O'Neill in a dispute over a game of cards.

Mail services, always a ready topic for the newspaper staff, were advertised. The National Mail and Transportation Company reassured readers of its connection by stagecoach to Tucson, 615 miles away. The Star Line stagecoach company advertised mail service west to Prescott, 475 miles away. Mail from the East came most of the way by train to Las Vegas,

Santa Fe 1880

New Mexico, sixty miles east of Santa Fe. However, the newspaper notified subscribers that until a more reliable arrival of news dispatches from the East was available, it could not resume its daily publication. Meanwhile, it would be a weekly, with some pages printed in Spanish.

The archbishop still languished on his sickbed. The Sisters of Charity, who ran the small hospital or clinic nearby, would have been ever so much better at nursing the gravely ill bishop, for they were trained as nurses. But he insisted the Sisters of Loretto were his preference. Even so, at one point, when he refused to take medicine as prescribed, it was a stalwart Sister from the hospital who entered his room and forced him to comply.

She was the no-nonsense Sister Blandina. People always did as Sister Blandina directed, or suffered the consequences! In this case, she noted in her diary that the bishop "soon recovered" after she got him to take his medicine. But it would take until early March for the elderly cleric to resume some of his normal routine—and that with little of his former vitality.

Sister Blandina Segale, named Rosa Maria by her parents, was born in Cicagna, near the city of Genoa, in Italy. Her birth was in the same year, 1850, that Archbishop Lamy left Ohio for the distant frontier territory of New Mexico as its first bishop. When she was four years old, her family moved to America, settling in Cincinnati to be among the large Italian immigrant community there. The city was also center for Catholic training and mission; the motherhouse for the Sisters of Charity was located there.

As a child, she observed the Sisters of Charity at work around Cincinnati. She heard how they even risked their lives to nurse soldiers on the field during the Civil War. She admired their courage and bravery. One day, to her father's surprise, she announced: "As soon as I am old enough, I shall be a Sister of Charity!" At sixteen, she entered the Sisters of Charity motherhouse and became known as Sister Blandina. It was September 13, 1866. Her older sister, Maria Maddelena, also joined the Sisters of Charity that month and took the spiritual name Sister Justina.

Sister Blandina heard that the Sisters of Charity had started a new mission out west, in Santa Fe, only the year before, and it was her dream to become part of that mission. That dream eventually became a reality, but only after a couple of detours. She was first posted to Fayetteville and Glendale, Ohio. Then she was ordered back to the motherhouse with her Sister to help reconvert the Italians of Cincinnati.

She was somewhat surprised when in December 1872, at age twenty-two, she received instructions to leave at once for Trinidad. She quickly confided to her sister that she was being sent to a happy island destination in the

Left: Archbishop Jean-Baptiste Lamy. Photograph taken sometime between 1875 and 1880. *Courtesy Palace of the Governors Photo Archives (NMHM/DCA) Negative 065116.*

Right: Sister Blandina Segale of the Sisters of Charity. Photograph taken sometime between 1870 and 1880. *Courtesy Palace of the Governors Photo Archives (NMHM/DCA) Negative 067735.*

Caribbean. Shortly thereafter, however, she discovered she was not going south, but west, indeed, to Trinidad, but in southern Colorado!

To arrive at her destination, she would travel by overland train to Kansas, then construction train to the end of the tracks and then by stagecoach into Colorado. Two well-wishing gentlemen, who traveled frequently in the west, tried to warn her about the harsh conditions she would encounter. They were Miguel Antonio Otero and John Perry Sellar, owners of the stage line serving Trinidad.

First, they warned her that she could easily become snowbound out on the prairies if she traveled in winter. But the real danger, they said, was cowboys. "No virtuous woman is safe near a cowboy!" She did not catch their meaning. "Why should snow or cowboys frighten me any more than others who will be traveling the same way?" she asked her sister.

Recalling that final part of the trip, she said, "For the first time I had indefinable fears. The cowboys were constantly in my mind. I expected there would be a number traveling with me on the plains. 'Snow-bound and

Santa Fe 1880

Stagecoaches like *Mountain Pride* were the main mode of transportation to areas not served by the railroad. *Photograph by William H. Roberts; courtesy of the Palace of the Governors Photo Archives (NMHM/DCA) negative 149888.*

cowboys' came in thought to annoy me." During the journey of a day and a night, her fear and the jostling of the stagecoach eliminated her appetite. She could not eat a thing, although the coach stopped several times at roadside stations for meals.

For most of the journey she was a lone traveler. Then one night around midnight, her ultimate fear was realized. The stage driver announced that she would have a traveling companion for some miles. "In the open door, by the light of a lantern, I saw a tall, lanky, Hoosier-like man, wearing a broad brimmed hat. On one arm he had a buffalo robe. While I sat riveted, he got in—asked me if I would take part of his 'kiver,' and before my fright permitted me to speak, he placed part of the buffalo robe over the comforter that enwrapped me, and sat beside me on the rear seat."

As she sat in mortal fright, she remembered the parting words of the archbishop back in Cincinnati, "Angels guard your steps." Would she make it to Trinidad alive? "The agony endured cannot be written. The silence and suspense unimaginable." All of a sudden, she started. The cowboy spoke:

"Madam!"

"Sir!"

"What kind of lady be you?"

"A Sister of Charity."

"Whose sister?"

"Everyone's Sister, a person who gives her life to do good to others."

"Quaker like, I reckon?"

"No, not quite."

She confided to her sister in her diary, "By this time I learned from his tone of voice that I had nothing to fear…I asked him why he became a cowboy. He said he had read of cowboys and ran away from home to become one."

"Is your mother still living?" she asked.

"Yes, I allow she is—leastwise she was when I left home six years ago."

"Have you written to her?"

"No, madam, and I allow that's beastly."

"It is certainly unkind to one whom you can always trust and who, I am sure, loves you as much now as she did when you were a little fellow."

His voice got husky. "What do you say I otter do?"

"Write; do so as soon as you get off this stage. Tell her you will soon make her a visit, and see to it that you keep your word."

"I will, so help me God! I was might feared to speak to you when I got in, because the mule driver said you was more particular than any lady he ever seen. I allow I am powerful glad I spoke to you."

The conversation made her feel more like a woman than ever before! "To think that this lubberly, good-natured cowboy had made me undergo such mortal anguish. He got off on the outskirts of Trinidad where the driver stopped to point out to me dugouts at the side of the foothills. 'This, lady, is Trinidad.' "

Shortly after her arrival, she vowed to start keeping a diary to journal her experiences for her sister, who years later followed in her footsteps to serve in Trinidad. It is her written record that reveals so much about her character, her grit, her curiosity and her ability to deal with the human condition. She served in that Colorado community for four years and in the process built a school, met Billy the Kid and learned to speak Spanish.

She could not know at the time but those very experiences would serve her well when she finally arrived in Santa Fe, where she eventually served for most of five years. This story is not only about her experiences in the capital city; it is also about that remarkable year, 1880; the year Santa Fe came of age.

2
Frontier Politics

The Democrats have never done any good to Santa Fe County in the management of its finances or its general affairs, and all the boasts of past commendable actions are but lies; while their promises of future good conduct cannot but be looked upon with suspicion in the light of their former broken promises and mal administration.
—The Santa Fe New Mexican, *October 24, 1880*

As the cold January days of 1880 wore on, Santa Fe was abuzz. Rumor had it that the railroad would arrive by mid-February. When citizens picked up their *Santa Fe New Mexican* in mid-January, the rumors were confirmed. The tracks were already at Cañocito, just twenty-two miles from town! The crews had obviously crested Glorieta Pass, that famous scene of the Civil War battle and one of the most difficult terrains of the entire track between Kansas and Santa Fe. It followed the path of the old Santa Fe Trail around the southern end of the Rocky Mountains, just southeast of Santa Fe. The newspaper also announced that the railroad company had "with business tact and evident fairness, left the location of our depot to our citizens of the town."

Anxious to accommodate the wishes of railroad officials, the city fathers quickly donated a forty-acre tract for the depot ground and buildings. Finally, Santa Fe would become known to the world. And more, the depot would be conveniently located no more than a mile from the town square, the Santa Fe Plaza.

With all the excitement about the railroad's soon arrival, the annual territorial legislative session that was about to begin got little notice. The citizen legislature, as mandated by the territorial constitution, met every year in mid-January: the legislators served without pay. New laws would be enacted and a highlight was the governor's State of the Territory address.

As the lawmakers began arriving from the far reaches of the territory, they were dismayed at the hustle and bustle of their once sleepy capital city. So many people in the streets. And prices for everything sky-high. Rooms were hard to find, much less a house to rent. And wood for the fireplace to keep you warm for the duration of the session: five to eight dollars per wagonload! Or one could buy it by the pound at eighteen to twenty-two cents. The capital city was expensive!

When the legislature gathered to organize for the session, the lower house took contentious sides. The governor reported to the secretary of the interior: "The lower house, thirteen Republicans to thirteen Democrats, had some difficulty in organizing. The struggle was for the Speakership, each party seeking to avail itself of contested seats. I took no part in the affair until the evening of the second day, when I invited the leaders of both sides to my office to consult about the situation. As they responded willingly, I had no trouble in effecting a compromise."

When they were finally organized, Governor Wallace rose to speak to the assembly. He announced an act of Congress that set the territorial legislature at 36 members, 24 in the house and 12 in the senate. As non-salaried members, their per diem would be reimbursed at four dollars a day plus mileage, but the Speaker of the house and the president of the senate would receive two dollars extra. Furthermore, federal guidelines mandated legislative districts at 12 of equal population, "except Indians not taxed."

With housekeeping items out of the way, Wallace went on to outline the challenges facing the territory. County boundaries were in need of reform; "some residents don't even know what county they live in!" He went on, "The laws are a masterpiece of confusion!" Towns needed

General Lew Wallace, governor of New Mexico from 1878 to 1881. *Engraving after a photograph by Napoleon Sarony; courtesy Palace of the Governors Photo Archives (NMHM/DCA) Negative 013123.*

incorporation. The criminal code needed revising. There was no territorial penitentiary. Although the legislature back in 1874 created the position of superintendent of schools, English was not yet taught in all schools.

Finally, he approached the most distressing of his present woes: the marauding Indians. He identified four distinct tribes: Navajo, Apache, Utes and Pueblos. Of the four, he claimed, the Apaches are the most troublesome; they are "cunning, blood thirsty, untamable." He declared the government must defend the people from these predators.

"It is unfortunate that your session is so limited by law," the governor continued. "Not to speak of new measures, the statutes requiring reform are so many and so important that thrice forty days might be profitably occupied in the work." With limited time and so much to do, he urged the lawmakers to consider wisely what items were most important. "Devote your selves to the consideration of a few laws most essential to the public welfare," he advised.

"To my surprise," he later wrote to his wife, "my message has given great satisfaction. I had a mixed audience of ladies and gentlemen, and when I had finished reading...I received what I never heard before during the delivery of a message—applause!"

As debates and arguments filled the legislative hall, word came that the Apaches were raiding and stealing stock on the Pecos, Delaware and Black Rivers in the south. A party of prospectors in the area was attacked, one killed, another two wounded. The rest took refuge at Fort Cummings, near Socorro on the Rio Grande. Two Indians were killed and others wounded. It was assumed they were from the Mescalero Apache Reservation, near Fort Sumner in Lincoln County. The lawmakers learned of a battle at the headwaters of the Rio Percha where six Indians were killed. It was estimated that there were currently three hundred Indians threatening the town of Hillsboro.

The legislature responded to the governor's appeals by appropriating $100,000 for the Army to clear the Apache menace in the south. General Edward Hatch, head of the U.S. Army headquarters in Santa Fe, had just returned from Colorado, where he dealt with the threat of a Ute uprising. He reported that there seemed to be calm in that area for now.

To compound the incoming news, word arrived that Billy the Kid had shot and killed one Joe Grant. Grant, a gunman and bounty hunter, decided to bring in Billy in hopes of claiming a major reward for doing so. But the Kid got the better of him, shot him first. Grant died on January 10.

Portal (porch) of the Palace of the Governors in 1880. *Photograph by William Henry Jackson; courtesy of the Palace of the Governors Photo Archives (NMHM/DCA) negative 118547.*

Santa Fe 1880

The Palace of the Governors where the 1880 legislature met. This sketch was made in the early 1880s. *A negative taken from an etching in* Illustrated New Mexico *3rd Edition by William G. Ritch; courtesy of the Palace of the Governors Photo Archives (NMHM/DCA) Negative 011212.*

While the world stormed around her, Sister Blandina continued tending the sick and wounded at the little St. Vincent Hospital, making beds, emptying bedpans and generally making sure the city's only medical facility was functioning as well as it could with limited resources. Railroad workers were her latest patients. With the tracks only a few miles away, the crews naturally found her hospital the logical place to bring their sick and wounded. She heard of one man who had been run over by a construction train car. He was so badly injured that a doctor in nearby Las Vegas immediately began amputations, but he died in the process and his body was shipped back to Kansas City.

To her own hospital came a man with a temperature of 105. The physician who brought him demanded a ten-dollar fee for the favor. The man was too sick to even understand what was requested. Sister Blandina reached into her own pocket and pulled out a ten-dollar bill. As she handed it over, she said, "Do not bring any more patients until your credentials are presented to the hospital authorities." This lady was in charge! The hospital's chief physician was Dr. Robert Longwell. He, more than anyone, appreciated her dedication. To help her cope with the many demands, he instituted a policy of discharging patients in three days once they no longer required bed rest.

Sister Blandina instituted her own regimen for patients who were well enough to be mobile. She ordered wood by the cord and set up a chopping yard next to the hospital. She assigned men to chop wood for five minutes a turn, to develop their stamina in view of their soon departure from the hospital. The male patients understood her goal of helping them regain their strength, all except one. An Irishman from the north of Ireland stood up in the convalescent ward to give a speech.

"Men, when that little boss comes in again and tells any of us to go to the wood pile to chop wood flatly say, 'No, I am a patient. You receive plenty of money, or else you would not go on the plains and grading camps to hunt for the sick!'"

As soon as she heard about it, Sister Blandina moved immediately to quell the mutiny. She took the bull by the horns: "I understand that someone here has advised the men not to chop wood when I ask them to do so?"

The culprit stood up, "I am the man who told the men not to chop wood, and that you are well paid for what you do, or else you would not go hunting for the sick."

She responded: "Suppose you put this question to every man in this ward, beginning with yourself, 'How much have you paid since you were received into the hospital?'"

The big man replied, "I did not pay anything—you did not ask me to."

"No, sir, you were too ill when we found you on the Santa Fe Trail. You may put the same question to any patient in the hospital." She then explained that going to the wood pile for five minutes was to help the patients regain their strength, prepare them for returning to work.

"I'll be hanged, Sister! I thought you were making money on us. I am a brute and could not understand why not a man here agreed with me. I will take my bundle and start on the road."

Having made herself clear, she said, "Good-bye, and God speed you."

One afternoon, twelve injured men were brought in from the rail works. They had been working in a cut at Apache Canyon, the very canyon where the U.S. Army marched triumphantly into Santa Fe during the Mexican-American War. The rails were now closing in on the city. The injured men were caught in a blast triggered by a fuse that went off prematurely. The Sisters scrambled to find enough beds for the newcomers. They ended up giving their own mattresses to accommodate the suffering men.

To top off her day, at 6:00 p.m., Sister Blandina saw flames on the chimney above the rooms where the recent patients had been settled. "Mother of Mercy, help us!" she shouted and sprang into action. She ran to

Santa Fe 1880

Burro loaded with firewood in the Santa Fe Plaza in the 1880s. *Photograph by Dana B. Chase; courtesy of the Palace of the Governors Photo Archives (NMHM/DCA) negative 005508.*

the convalescent ward and organized those men who could stand up to form a bucket brigade. "Marvel how composedly I acted, because the thought uppermost in my mind was that the last patients will be cremated if the fire is not extinguished," she later recalled.

She was able to climb a ladder up onto the roof of the first story section of the building where she had a good view of the blaze. She yelled down to the men below and ordered two of them to put a third man on their shoulders so they could hand up salt and water. "I threw the salt down the chimney. The sparks rushed out, but the blaze subsided. Water was handed to me in the same manner. I poured one bucket down the chimney and nothing came out but black smoke; the fire was extinguished!"

She was strong enough through the emergency, but when the fire was out, she began trembling, felt weak and sat down on the roof to recover. Suddenly, she heard the voice of Dr. John Symington asking how in the world she got up on the roof.

"Diving quickly into psychic phenomena I knew I had been the subject of mind over matter. Dr. Symington belongs to the volunteer Bucket Brigade. After looking around a few seconds he did not refer to the subject again. I doubt not the men think I'm either a saint or a witch."

Soon after that event, she had an interesting political encounter. "I never speak of politics or the acts of politicians, but I consider this incident worth while," she wrote her sister. "There are two political parties here, Republicans and Democrats. The first party goes by the name the 'Santa Fe Ring.' This party has been doing things to suit themselves, so the Democrats say."

The Santa Fe Ring was a political and economic machine headed by several prominent lawyers and city leaders in Santa Fe. They invested in mining and cattle and were deeply involved in land grant issues, mostly in Colfax County, where land boundaries were contestable. They often won their cases because fellow members of the Santa Fe Ring occupied important judicial offices.

One of the men known to be in the group approached one day and predicted a Democratic candidate would most likely come see her with promises to help in her work. As predicted, the contender for his seat on the county commission came to visit. "The Democrats expect their whole ticket to be elected," he began. "I'm going to be a true friend to you, Sister!" She assured the gentleman that "whatever you do for me will be for the benefit of those whom we serve."

Up to this point, Santa Fe County had been paying the hospital eight dollars to cover the burial cost for every indigent patient who died. Considering that the Sisters prepared each body for burial, procured a gravesite and had it dug, made the coffin and transported the body to its resting place, that eight dollars covered only a fraction of the cost.

Not long after the visit of the politician, Sister Blandina was doing some errands in town and took the opportunity to stop by the new commissioner's place of business; he owned a store in the heart of the city. It happened that he heard about a recent burial and inquired as to how much it cost to bury a man. "I used the prisoners to do the work," she replied, "but still it cost the county $30," the amount collected for burying Santa Fe citizens as opposed to the eight dollars granted for burying the homeless.

The conversation continued, "Just because I am chairman of the County Commissioners I must economize. Now, Sister, do as you have been doing—charge the county $8," Trying to hide her anger, she replied, "It cannot be done," and she went on her way. When she returned to the hospital, she was told a homeless man had just died. She returned to the commissioner and announced the death and asked, "Will you allow $15 for his burial?"

"Now Sister, you must help me to economize. Bury him for what you have been receiving, $8." She answered, "In fifteen minutes the corpse will be brought to your office. You can economize as you wish. Good-bye." She had barely walked forty steps when she heard him call behind her: "Sister! We will allow you $15 for the burial of each poor patient." With that remark, the commissioner unknowingly became a member of Sister Blandina's own "Ring!"

3
A Trade School for Girls

Mark Twain? Ah, yes, I remember—he was the ignorant American who asked if the Egyptian mummies were dead and who did not know who Christopher Columbus was. Strange how his education could have been so neglected.
—Archibald Forbes, quoted in the Santa Fe New Mexican, *December 5, 1880*

If running a hospital was not enough to keep the Sisters of Charity busy, they also ran a small orphanage for abandoned and otherwise needy children. They conducted classes for them in a small building next to the hospital. The first assignment for Sister Blandina back when she arrived in Santa Fe was to see what she could do to improve the school for the children. Based on her experience building a school in Trinidad, she immediately became head teacher. Soon, poorer families in town heard of the school and started sending their children, too.

Her superior approached her one day; "Most Rev. Archbishop Lamy thinks one great need in the Territory is a Trade School for girls. Now, sister, will you undertake to build it?"

"How much money have we with which to begin building?"

"Nothing, Sister. Do as you did in Trinidad. I was told you had not a cent when you started to build your adobe schoolhouse, and you finished it without debts...use your originality as you did elsewhere, and with God's blessing you will get through."

She recalled her experience in Trinidad. The low adobe building that served as a school in that distant town was dank, dark and musty, in great

The Sisters' Industrial School, nearly finished in background, and St. Francis Cathedral under construction in foreground, 1880. *Photograph by Ben Wittick; courtesy of the Palace of the Governors Photo Archives (NMHM/DCA) negative 015857.*

need of refurbishment. She decided to appeal to the pride of the locals by taking matters into her own hands; she climbed up on the roof and started removing the adobe bricks with both hands! When a woman who wielded considerable power in the community became alarmed at seeing the Sister doing the heavy work on her own, she quickly organized a crew of men to come take over the job.

But how could she start such a project in Santa Fe? Then she remembered her encounter with an accomplished architect in town. Projectus Mouly was the son of the architect and stonemason Antoine Mouly, imported from France by the archbishop to build the cathedral and a chapel for the Sisters of Loretto some years before. The elder Mouly became blind while working on the church and returned to Europe, but his son Projectus remained to complete the two buildings.

However, as the projects got well underway, certain clergy criticized his work. They wanted him to make changes that, in his opinion, would spoil the architectural beauty of the buildings. A lover of art, he would not submit to changes he felt would be an inferior plan, so he resigned.

Sister Blandina immediately thought of the young artist. She asked him to come to the convent. "I saw at once he was strangely touched that I should send for him. I told him my plans for building an Industrial School. Was it the extreme pressure of mental distress being experienced by this young genius, or his determination to get away from what he believes would be his ultimate downfall, or my enthusiasm in plunging into a great undertaking requiring large sums of money and not a cent on hand, that made him say 'I'm with you, Sister, when do you wish to begin?' " At that moment, he willingly became a member of Sister's growing "Ring" of supporters.

With little money and no workers, Sister Blandina convinced the clerics who presided over Sunday services to make an appeal for volunteer workers. A number of men showed up, and in a short time, foundations were laid.

Critics questioned the sanity of such a project. "How can a building sixty feet high, and a cupola on top of that, stand? The first big wind will blow it down." Others feared if the adobe walls were not made properly, the rains would melt them down. Plans called for a three-story building, one of the largest in the city.

"So many were the criticisms on the building that the Vicar-General said to me one day: 'Sister, you remind me of the crocodile, which looks to neither right nor left, but makes straight for its prey.' I confess my ignorance, I do not see the analogy," she wrote her sister.

New Mexicans who had traveled or otherwise experienced life outside the territory became her best supporters. "The others, who are afraid something disastrous will happen to the building which was erected under the most peculiar circumstances, are those who have not seen anything but one-story adobe buildings and mud roofs." In time, her team started a brickyard, opened its own rock quarry, secured a source for lime and had its lumber hand-sawed by local carpenters.

As the source behind the force, Sister Blandina became director of the overall project. Constantly busy, she wore many hats. One of her fellow Sisters proudly accredited her with many titles; she introduced her as the "Elder Sister," "The Sister of the Sheep" and "The Sister of the Lumber."

She wrote, "I have had as many adjective names as are the names of the material we have used, though we did not use sheep in the building—but we did use sheep to pay off some of the workmen…there is certainly no monotony in our work." She had every hope that the school might open within the year.

Another school, less grandiose than Sister Blandina's, already was taking in students. Flora Spiegelberg, the wife of a leading Jewish merchant, organized a small school that winter.

> *I organized the first non-sectarian school, one room in an old adobe house, very primitive. I made it obligatory that the ten children be taught to recite the Ten Commandments. Early in 1880…I collected $1,000 from the old pioneer merchants and Federal officials for the purpose of building a modern school house.*

More than that, she cajoled General Hatch into gaining federal approval for utilizing one acre of government land near Fort Marcy as the site for the new school. Now she was searching for ways to fund her project.

> *Mr. Smith, the contractor, who was very anxious to build my new home and the store for the Spiegelberg brothers, was told that he could not obtain these two contracts unless he was willing to build a one-story frame school house with many windows to let in sunshine, and also modern desks and benches. After some hesitation, he finally agreed for the sum of $1,000 to have this school building ready for the first week in September. The children were very happy in the two large schoolrooms.*
>
> *I also organized the first Children's Gardens. I taught them how to cultivate flowers and vegetables…I also gave the children nature study lessons: aided by a magnifying glass I showed a large collection of all kinds of insects and how the golden, yellow pollen carried on the tiny hairs of their wings while flitting from flower to flower dropped on the pistils of the various flowers…I also taught the children sewing and fancy needlework. I gave a weekly medal for general excellence.*

While the school projects were under way, news came to the capital that Chief Vitorio and his band had returned to the territory from Mexico and were again on the rampage in the south. Their winning strategy was to cross the border when things got hot on one side, then return to the other side when conditions were relaxed. He knew neither Mexico nor the United States permitted its troops to cross into the other's territory.

Governor Wallace and General Hatch, with the funds provided by the legislature, were ready to launch a force against Vitorio. Their vanguard would be the U.S. 9th Cavalry, stationed at Santa Fe's Fort Marcy military compound. The 9th consisted of the famous buffalo soldiers, black troops sent to Santa Fe in 1876 to be peacekeepers in the western territories. In 1871, the Comanche bestowed the name of an animal they revered, the buffalo, on the men of the 10th Cavalry because they were impressed with their toughness in battle. The black troops seemingly accepted the name with pride.

The latest raid by Indians came from the area of the Pecos, Delaware and Black Rivers, where a party of prospectors was attacked. One was killed, two were wounded. Two Indians were killed and others wounded. The miners took refuge at Fort Cummings. It was surmised that this attack might again have been by a band of Mescalero Apaches, not Vitorio's band. At the same time, twenty horses were stolen from a ranch south of Las Cruces, and they were trailed to the Mescalero Apache Reservation. But no further action was taken, as the ranchers could not lawfully enter the reservation.

Major Albert Morrow, a likeable white officer of the 9th Cavalry who made many friends in Santa Fe, led the soldiers in this latest action. They located the Indians near the headwaters of the Puerco River and had several skirmishes with them but eventually Vitorio vanished into thin air. In the process, three soldiers were killed and seven wounded.

Hearing the news, General Hatch predicted it would take two months to teach the Indians a "lesson they will not forget." His optimism may have come from a new directive from the War Department: it granted permission for his troops to enter Indian reservations to punish them on their own ground.

In other news, the *Santa Fe New Mexican* reported that Congress had passed a Land Grant Bill. It provided ascertainment and settling of private land claims. Its importance to the territory was evident by full front-page coverage in the newspaper. It no doubt would affect the maneuverings of the Santa Fe Ring. And the newspaper

General Edward Hatch said it would take two months to teach the Indians a "lesson they will not forget." *Clipart courtesy FCIT, https://etc.usf.edu/clipart.*

Santa Fe 1880

The 9th Cavalry Band, made up of the buffalo soldiers, on the Santa Fe Plaza in 1880. *Photograph by Ben Wittick; courtesy of the Palace of the Governors Photo Archives (NMHM/DCA) Negative 050887.*

carried a brief note about one of the last actions of the recent territorial legislative session: it passed a bill permitting cousins to marry!

Another major breaking story was about an attempt to rob an express train at Las Vegas. Thieves from Texas, including Thomas House, William Randall and John Dorsey, were apprehended in the act by Marshal Joe Carson. A gunfight ensued, and the city marshal and Randall were shot and

The archbishop's residence in Santa Fe, believed to be the first St. Vincent's Hospital run by the Sisters of Charity. *Photograph by Bennett and Brown; courtesy of the Palace of the Governors Photo Archives (NMHM/DCA) negative 015266.*

killed. Carson himself was a member of the Dodge City gang that early the previous year had moved to Las Vegas to begin a new chapter in life and he became city marshal.

The surviving robbers were put in the city jail. But their lives ended seventeen days later when a lynching mob stormed the jail and took them out to be hanged. This at the same time the *Santa Fe New Mexican* announced a new invention for using electricity for executions. A German writer described it as a "ceremony of execution…to shock the wretch into the next world."

Sister Blandina was well acquainted with death. She described one of many occasions when she conducted a burial:

> *A convalescent and myself lowered somebody's darling into a coffin. I borrowed a wagon and made a round of the hospital to find patients available to accompany the corpse with me to the graveyard. The only available help I could get was a weak patient to drive, a one-legged man who carried a crutch and a one-armed man.*

The funeral cortege started. "All went well until we had to carry the coffin. The mules were skittish, so the old man stayed with the wagon while the one-legged and the one-armed man were asked to carry the light part of the coffin. I took the heavy weight."

Since no vehicles were allowed in the graveyard, the three coffin bearers had to carry it from the wagon across a stretch of land to the gravesite. "I exercised my will to the limit so as not to let the coffin drop. But suddenly my sight left me." Nevertheless, she was able to stumble blindly forward until they reached the burial spot. "I was on the point of telling the two men that I had lost my sight, when I saw as quickly as I had been deprived of sight. Of course, weakness was the cause."

As she walked back to the hospital, an agent of the Atchison, Topeka & Santa Fe Railway saw her and asked her to step into his office. In the office were four officials of the company. One asked what she had been doing. "Burying a dead man," was her reply. "Couldn't someone else do it?" he asked. "Possibly," she replied. The man said, "Just let me know, Sister, when I can do anything for you." Her "Ring" was growing!

4
Chasing Vitorio

Those Indians who have been previously taught that the highest aim of a good Indian should be to become civilized, learn to read, plough and abstain from swearing, are now peremptorily told that their highest and safest aim is to learn to behave themselves, the time for the absorbing of that lesson being also limited.
—The Santa Fe New Mexican, *July 2, 1880*

Chief Vitorio was feeling the heat from Major Morrow's troops as January 1880 came to a close. The chase was taking place day and night amid rumors that Vitorio wanted to surrender. He was surprised in an attack by the buffalo soldiers at his camp on Sierra Mateo, twenty miles south of Monica Springs. Morrow was heard to say he wanted to take Vitorio captive and would pursue him to that end. The chief barely escaped the raid, but the soldiers captured one hundred horses and mules from his quickly abandoned camp.

Vitorio had no way of knowing it, but the game plan by the military was about to change. The government of Mexico officially agreed to work with the United States to hunt down the renegade. Even more, Mariano, head war chief of the Navajos, offered to go on the warpath against Vitorio. The military accepted the offer.

But just when Morrow thought he had the upper hand, a scouting party from Vitorio's band attacked a supply train headed for the trooper's camp. The wagons from Santa Fe were delivering thirty thousand rounds of ammunition, ten thousand rations and forage for the Army's steeds. Escorts from the 9th Cavalry out of Fort Marcy repulsed the Indians. Two soldiers were injured in the skirmish, and a Navajo scout was killed.

Vitorio and his band were forced south to the famous Jornada del Muerte, the "Journey of Death," that detoured east of the Rio Grande, where mountains and canyons made travel along the riverside impossible. Noting his southward direction, the Mexican army was alerted that he might try to escape across the border again.

The Indian chief was not the only culprit the government was chasing. Billy the Kid was stirring up trouble again in Lincoln County. "Billy the Kid is using his gun freely. The people of the territory are aroused and demand his capture, dead or alive. Rewards have been offered for his capture," wrote Sister Blandina. "Our Governor, Lewis Wallace, has shown heroic bravery by going to Lincoln County to try to pacify the storm. He had a number of interviews with Billy but to no avail. New rewards have been offered both by the Governor and the people."

The problem was especially acute for the governor; the wild gangs in Lincoln County controlled much of what happened there. Conditions were so out of control and the gang wars so common that there seemed no way to bring law and order to the place. It was war in Lincoln County! "The United

Buffalo soldiers from the 10th Cavalry in camp at an unknown location. *Photograph by Henry A. Schmidt; courtesy of the (NMHM/DCA) negative 049017.*

Apache chief Vitorio. *Drawing by Clarence Batchelor; courtesy of the Palace of the Governors (MNM/DCA) negative 2109.*

States marshal told me that he had a large number of warrants which he dared not serve, and could not find deputies rash enough to attempt service, when they knew their lives would pay the penalty," said Wallace.

The governor lamented his inability to effect more control and order in the territory: "I wish my successor, whoever he be, was come. Of course he will do just as I did, have the same ideas, make the same attempts, and with the same heartiness of effort, soon cool in the zeal, then finally say, 'All right, let her drift.' Every calculation based on experience elsewhere fails in New Mexico."

The only way to quell the madness, he decided, was to appeal to the president for assistance. "The military commander at Fort Stanton sent a list of the murders that had been committed...I forwarded these combined statements to President Hayes, and asked him to proclaim an insurrection in New Mexico, which he did. That was the only way for me to have the use of the troops for the purposes I desired." The U.S. Army command at Santa Fe now had war on two fronts.

Back in Santa Fe itself, the pace of life was picking up speed as the colder winter months came to an end. At the newspaper office, the staff was gearing up to begin launching its daily edition again. With the likelihood of better service by train in a few days when the tracks reached the city, they were optimistic that incoming information from the East would increase sufficiently to fill the pages.

Social life in the city was picking up as well. A benefit bazaar for St. Thomas Church had invaded the Palace of the Governors. The newspaper reported, "Governor Wallace retreated from his rooms in the Palace upon invasion of the fair sex," who were in charge. The event launched with a performance of the 9th Cavalry brass band. On sale were oysters, cakes, candy and toy dolls.

A baile, or dance, on the outskirts of town organized by Maximo Martinez was going well one night until three drunken interlopers, Dick Moore, Henry Collins and Banjo Charley, arrived. A ruckus commenced, and guns were drawn. One Curley Moore was shot in the thigh. He was treated on the scene but died from loss of blood.

The editor colorfully related another story in the newspaper: "A Chinaman presented himself at the county clerk's office this morning about 9 o'clock to obtain a license to marry an Indian squaw. The Chinaman claims to be 35 years old, while the lucky maiden is 23. It has long been claimed by scientists that the Indian is a descendant of the Chinese, and the coming together of these two might be productive."

Noting the uniqueness of the situation, the editor went on to say, "We believe that this is the first instance of the kind that has happened since the Chinese have invaded our coast. It is only another result, however, that John Chinaman intends to settle down to business, as he is picking up all the stray maidens he can capture throughout the state."

Probably the most exciting news in town was that an agent of Mitchell's Star Dramatic Company arrived to make arrangements for performances by the drama troupe. Its first production would be *Star of the West*, with Millie Willard taking the part of Lucretia Borgia.

Sister Blandina could not be bothered by latest events. With her school project and duties at the hospital, she had little time for frivolities. "The Reverend Antonio Fourchegu came this morning and said: 'Sister, I want to help you a little. I am going to turn over to the credit of the Sisters of Charity 600 ewes, bringing 25 percent interest yearly, and a two thousand dollar note, bearing 10 per cent interest, which you can claim very shortly… for these gifts I make the condition that I am to have a private room at St. Vincent Hospital…If I am not ill, I shall not come, but should I take sick, I want to secure a place to recover or go to God.'"

Thankful for this help, she secretly admitted him into her Ring. She recounted an experience they shared:

> *Galloping on the plains near Pecos, he saw a very strange looking animal—a quadruped! He determined to capture it. The animal ran swiftly away. Father Fourchegu followed till it was exhausted, when it backed against a tree, faced its pursuer, and with glaring eyes and sharp teeth, defended itself against its enemy, fighting and scratching furiously.*

He captured the savage animal and wrapped his coat around it. Then he discovered it was a little girl!

> *Father Fourchegu brought the child to us. With great difficulty we subdued her, cut her long, tangled hair, her long nails, and dressed her like the other girls. She retained that frightened look and propensity to scratch and to dig into the ground. At first she could not speak, only grunt, but in time she learned to speak also.*
>
> *Some years before, a little girl had disappeared. The parents thought she was dead. When the girl was brought to us she was the talk of the day. People came from far and near to see the wild girl. The newspapers had broadcasted the fact. Then came a man and his wife to see the child. They recognized her as their little daughter, Carmela, who had disappeared several years before!*

Sister Blandina was, by this time, a paragon of information and authority on charitable matters. One day, the Sister in charge of the kitchen came to her room, very perplexed: "Sister, we have not a handful of vegetables to prepare for dinner, and seventy-two patients, thirty-five orphans, and sixteen Sisters to feed. Please figure it out, you, who, I have been told, are never daunted!"

"The problem will be solved in ten minutes," Sister Blandina assured her.

The only way she could think of remedying the situation was to prevail upon the generosity of the archbishop. "I went to the rear of our empty vegetable garden and looked over the adobe wall into the Archbishop's garden. There I saw an abundance of cabbage, turnips, carrots, and what not. Most of the vegetables were buried heads down in the ground, roots showing above ground.

"I made one athletic spring (old habits die slowly) and landed near the cabbage patch. Throwing over into our vacant garden at least two dozen cabbage heads, I did the same with each of the other vegetables, only in greater number, as the sizes were smaller."

"Then I went to His Grace's door and rapped."

"Come in," he called.

"I have come to make a confession out of the confessional," she said meekly.

"My little Sister, what have you been doing?"

"Stealing, Your Grace. With never a thought of restitution, I dug up vegetables from your garden to last us three days."

"And then?"

"Whatever you say."

"Tell Louis to give you all there are."

"Thank you very much," is all she could say. "Shortly after this, Mr. Frank Manzanares, of the firm Browne and Manzanares, sent sacks of coffee and sugar. I think His Grace is guilty."

5
Santa Fe's Triumph

Very unexpectedly the news that the train was on time reached here yesterday afternoon and what is better still the report was more confirmed by its arrival at the depot five minutes before it was due. It was a pleasant surprise for everybody, and to be able to get the mail in a reasonable time was generally relished as a luxury.
—*The* Santa Fe New Mexican, *December 8, 1880*

In early February, the city was bursting with anticipation. The first train to arrive in the city was soon to appear. The people of Santa Fe assumed that the city would become a major stop on the rail line; after all, "Santa Fe" was in the railroad company's name! Much to their dismay, however, the engineers decided at the last minute to bypass the city lest it delay their forward thrust toward Albuquerque and points beyond. This decision caused shockwaves in the old city.

In a state of panic, the city leaders convinced the rail company to construct a feeder line to the new depot and agreed to raise funds to help pay for it. Travelers would forever have to alight at Galisteo Junction, eighteen miles south, and resettle into another train for the final leg of their journey into the city. But the excitement of finally seeing a train actually chug into town overcame the inconvenience of last-minute decisions.

As state and local officials assembled amid an immense crowd to witness the event, the last spike was driven at high noon on Monday, February 9. A parade assembled on the west side of the Santa Fe Plaza.

Santa Fe 1880

The Atchison, Topeka & Santa Fe engine known as *Baby* on the tracks at Glorieta Summit, 1880. *Photograph by Ben Wittick; courtesy of the Palace of the Governors Photo Archives (NMHM/DCA) negative 015780.*

The state marshal, on horseback, was in the lead, followed by the 9th Cavalry Band and territorial, county and federal officials. General Hatch and his staff, members of the territorial legislature, a college band, citizens and carriages followed.

At the depot, students from city schools lined the platform and the two bands were stationed on either side of the platform. To gain a vantage point, people climbed atop the depot roof or on top of their wagons and even on each other's shoulders. The officiating party consisted of General Hatch,

Chief Justice L. Bradford Prince, Governor Lew Wallace and Commissioner Abraham Staab. Chief Justice Prince gave a glowing speech heralding the long-awaited event.

The last railroad spikes were driven by the four leading officials. "These four, representatives of the citizens and military, stepped forth, and taking the hammers, with a few blows completed the railroad, amid the huzzas and loud applause of the spectators," reported the newspaper. "Monday was a glorious day for Santa Fe." It went on to predict "The completion of this railroad removes the last and only impediment to her rapid advance, and each day hereafter will see an increase of population and of wealth."

The people marveled at this incredible ceremony—so many months, for some years waiting for this glorious day. Only a dozen years before, people making the journey by stage from Missouri endured two weeks of discomfort, had miserable meals at irregular intervals and arrived exhausted in Santa Fe. Before stagecoach service, covered wagons took over two months to accomplish the task. The newspaper quipped that arriving passengers in those days were almost willing to spend the remainder of their lives in New Mexico rather than go through the same experience a second time.

Most people on this joyous occasion were oblivious to the more momentous meaning of the day; it was the end of Old Santa Fe Trail. The trail was done for. Now it would only be a romantic, nostalgic relic of the march of time and a study for armchair historians for centuries to come.

With the arrival of the railroad, life was rapidly changing, especially for Sister Blandina. Even before the first train arrived, she began seeing all kinds of strangers, mostly men, wander into town: "Consumptives, men with money looking to become millionaires, land-grabbers, experienced and inexperienced miners, quacks, professional deceivers, publicity men lauding gold mines that do not exist. I could use half a dozen more adjectives and yet not touch on all the methods of deception carried on."

She recalled an incident near Trinidad when unscrupulous land grabbers attempted to steal a coal mine that was about to make its owner rich. It was reported to the Sister by an informer that "the mine shows prospects of making its owner a millionaire in the very near future. Today a number of posts were placed in the first excavation. These can be shifted to such positions that when the boss and miners begin work tomorrow morning all the props will suddenly collapse…the two men who did this are desperadoes and will stop at nothing."

Sister Blandina recorded her response in her diary: "Realizing the deep significance of what he disclosed, I needed to reflect seriously. The two

Santa Fe 1880

Looking east at the Old Santa Fe Trail, where it entered Santa Fe, in 1880. The old trail went into disuse after serving fifty-nine years. *Photograph by H. Gurnsey, courtesy of the Palace of the Governors Photo Archives (NMHM/DCA) negative 011118.*

desperadoes—especially one of them, and this one controlled the mind of the other—were well known to me." She felt she could not go to the mine herself to intervene but she knew she had to act.

"Among my former pupils is a level-headed Indian. Mentally, I had already sent for him…his first question was, 'Qué, hay, Hermana?' (What is it Sister?) I answered: 'A big one this time. Workingmen are wanted at the mine—go to the boss and hire yourself this evening. Be the first at the mine in the morning. Bring your miner's light with you. Inspect the supports and call attention of the boss to anything that looks dangerous to you.' " Needless to say, the plot to cripple the mine was discovered. Sister Blandina saved the day.

The view that tired travelers in covered wagons would behold as they entered the city after traveling over two months across the prairies. *Photograph by William Henry Jackson; courtesy of the Palace of the Governors Photo Archives (NMHM/DCA) negative 054100.*

The Lamy railroad junction, presumably where the track financed by city leaders into town branched off from the main AT&SF line. *Photograph by J.R. Riddle; courtesy of the Palace of the Governors Photo Archives (NMHM/DCA) negative 076033.*

Santa Fe 1880

Now there was news in Santa Fe that the old turquoise mine at Chaichuitl Mountain, about ten miles south of town, would be reopened. This mine had a history. It is believed mining at this Cerrillos site began five hundred years before the arrival of Spanish explorer Coronado in 1540. In 1680, there was a cave-in, and many Indians working in the mine were killed. Some said nearly one hundred died.

The Spanish tried to force the Indians back to work but this in part sparked a Pueblo Indian Revolt that year, probably the most successful Indian revolt in the history of North America. Chief Popé, of the San Juan Pueblo, was the main instigator. That this mine might reopen was big news. Gold, silver, copper, lead, iron, coal and turquoise were being found at various sites around the New Mexico Territory. The promise of fast profits was attracting hundreds of miners and speculators to Santa Fe.

There was also a report that the Old Placer Mine, twenty-seven miles south, was sold to some Eastern capitalists. The nearby New Placer Mine was also to be sold. During the last couple years, $40,000–$250,000 worth of gold per year was mined in the two mines! Silver mines were also doing well; on one recent day, $12,000 of silver bricks from Grant County were being shipped East by train.

Sister Blandina, weary of miners' stories, turned her attention once more to the new school project. She continued to shoulder comments and criticisms of the building that was starting to take shape. Some of the moneyed women of the city were jealous of her success. One overheard conversation was a complaint that money going to the school could better be used to build some new homes in the city.

The president of San Miguel College saw the girl's school project as competition to a building program at his school. He feared Sister Blandina would soon be making a general appeal to the citizens for funds. This could impede his plans to start a $3,000 drive to cover the next payment on their new school building.

"Sister, do you intend to collect in Santa Fe to help you?"

"I have not given the subject a thought," she replied.

"Because if you expect to make a collection, I will temporarily have to stop work on the new college." He informed her that the college's vice president, Father Baldwin, was about to make a general appeal to local citizens.

"I am happy to tell you that none of us thought of soliciting in Santa Fe, perhaps the reason is that our people have been so wonderfully good to us."

"Well, Sister, I was misinformed."

"Please tell Brother Baldwin I wish him all the success his endeavor deserves."

In spite of the challenges, she continued to be optimistic about the school project. "We are drawing on amateur talent in Santa Fe for a concert we intend to give at the opening of the Industrial School. Mr. Wedles will preside at the piano. Mrs. Symington will give one number, a vocal solo. Our orphan girls will fill in the greater part of the programme," she wrote her sister.

Concerning Maria Teresa Symington, Sister Blandina paused in her school narrative to reflect on this lady's audacious background. She was married to the well-known medical doctor in town. "It is a well known fact that Mrs. Symington and the doctor were the actors in the largest romance ever enacted since the Spanish invasion."

It seems Mrs. Symington's family, the Armijos of Albuquerque, arranged a marriage for her with the son of a distinguished and rich family in Mexico. Sister Blandina stated:

> *Neither of the betrothed had ever met. The day for the wedding was set and both families were making elaborate preparations.*
>
> *The groom gathered his retinue in marching order, cavalry style, a coach drawn by a span of the best red horses decked in green and gold and all mountings solid silver—on horses and coach. The cavalcade approached the splendor of old-time princes going from one kingdom to another to claim a bride. A musical band rejoiced the travelers.*
>
> *When the groom and his followers arrived in Old Albuquerque (as the Spaniards express it) all the world turned out. The servants were told to prepare the bride-to-be to meet her affianced—the bride was nowhere to be seen! A note stated that she and Dr. Symington had gone to Santa Fe to be married!*

Years before, Dr. Symington, like so many travelers headed west, had followed the Santa Fe Trail as a teamster and landed in Old Albuquerque, where he met and fell in love with Miss Armijo. Now they were a happy couple in Santa Fe, part of the Blandina Ring. Sister Blandina, bemused by the incident, concluded, "The Doctor had his M.D. degree, but came out as a teamster for frolic and ended in marriage!"

6
Boom Times

Although usually an ordinary town, Santa Fe is burdened just now with a number of thieves and rogues, an affliction to which every town which has just secured the railroad, has to submit.
—*The* Santa Fe New Mexican, *February 21, 1880*

Now that the train had arrived, the *Santa Fe New Mexican* was bullish on the future of the city. The newspaper's exuberance could well be understood because it was about to begin daily editions. The editor claimed, "With this the New Mexican must and shall be a success." The newspaper boasted of having the first printing presses in New Mexico: several cylinder presses and seven power presses.

The first daily issue reported several of the downtown businesses were doing more than $1,500 a day in sales! With so much activity, the majority of stores on the plaza required clerks to sleep in the store at night. It was a precautionary measure. Lit only by candlelight, the shops were easy targets for characters of the night.

Very early one Saturday morning, two men were found fighting near the Santa Fe River. One said the other was his brother, and the second man said the first was trying to rob him. Both were taken and locked up in the city jail. The next morning, the mayor identified the two men as brothers, and "for his little slip of memory, the drunken man was fined five dollars plus costs!" said the newspaper.

The Atchison, Topeka & Santa Fe Railway depot in Santa Fe. *Courtesy of the Palace of the Governors Photo Archives (NMHM/DCA) negative 104466.*

Santa Fe 1880

Joe Palmer, proprietor of the Texas Saloon in town, got overly drunk one night between 7:00 and 8:00. He accosted citizens on San Francisco Street while brandishing a breech-loading shotgun. Finally, he was taken down by several pedestrians and hauled off to jail.

Another night, Dr. Longwell was walking by the jail and saw a huge hole cut through the wall. It opened onto the street. He gave the alarm. Deputy Sheriff Charles Conklin and jailer Enrique Silva set out to find the eight prisoners who had escaped. They quickly caught two: Frank Spain, who was in for murder, and William Clancy, jailed for robbing a stage. They confessed to making the hole in the wall with a pair of scissors and a spoon! It had taken them two weeks to accomplish the task. A week later, the sheriff captured another jailbird, murderer Dan Waterman. The officer tracked him and surprised him in his bed one night at a Mexican camp twenty-four miles from Santa Fe.

The Santa Fe jail was becoming more and more a focal point in town as the inmate population grew. Just when he was needed most, Police Officer Lindsley resigned his post. He said, "He could not afford to work with the small salary."

In other miscellany news, two horses were found fully bridled walking down San Francisco Street, known as the most active part of town for its entertainments and drinking establishments. The horses were put in a corral, where their owner found them the next morning. A lady's purse was found in the same area containing "two twenty dollar gold Mexican coins, one $20 greenback, one American trade dollar, three twenty-five cent coins and three or more gold dollars." The editor was waiting to hear from the rightful owner.

At the same time, social life for the gentry was pulsating. The 9th Cavalry band began performing two or three times a week in the plaza. The Mitchell Dramatic Company had its successful performance of *Star of the West*. According to the editor, it "with one bound leaped into popular favor." And the star, Millie Willard, showed "tigress spirit" as Lucretia Borgia. The company's next performance was announced, *Under the Gaslight*, something about which Santa Feans knew very little. The city still survived evenings with lighted candles. Gaslights were a wonder about which they could only dream.

It was announced that a new entertainment venue would soon open. Theatre Comique was to be inaugurated as a dance hall. It would feature "fair damsels from Kansas City" as dancers. There was even speculation that Santa Fe might one day have its own theater where legitimate plays could be performed.

A view of Santa Fe from the east in 1880. *Photograph by Ben Wittick; courtesy of the Palace of the Governors Photo Archives (NMHM/DCA) negative 015843.*

For the longtime locals, there were other entertainments. A race between a Mexican horse and an American horse found the Mexican to be the winner. The take-home purse was $200. Such challenges to race came along nearly every month.

Cockfighting, an age-old and cruel pastime, was deplored by Flora Spiegelberg in her remembrances:

> *Like bull fighting in Spain, so cockfights were a national game and pastime in New Mexico. Special breeds were carefully raised and well trained. Small, very sharp knives securely fastened to their feet, these cocks fought well, urged on by their owners and the cheering of the excited crowds. Often large sums of money were lost and won betting on which game cock could hold out the longest.*

Santa Fe 1880

The fights took place at the cockpit behind Bailey's Saloon on the plaza, at the corner of San Francisco Street. But these events were doomed: the legislature early in the year passed a law prohibiting it.

The "frivolities" of the city made Sister Blandina all the more determined to get her school built. Education, she was sure, would keep her schoolchildren from succumbing to the allures of the city streets. The recent arrival of the train gave her hope that materials from the East could more easily be obtained. Before the rails arrived, a large quantity of corrugated iron roofing was ordered. When it did arrive, it was discovered that it would be totally unsuitable for the roof of the school building. "Now Sister Augustine and myself will go on to St. Louis to purchase roof material and return with an expert man to put it on," Sister Blandina stated.

In a couple of weeks, the Sisters returned from St. Louis "with a workman who is an expert and will lay the slate on the Industrial School. Mr. Burke comes with the intention of doing prospecting work. This will exempt us from paying his expenses to return to St. Louis. Our roof will be the first slate roof in the territory."

"This morning I made a survey of the premises and missed the ten boxes of corrugated iron. Sister Louise was in charge of affairs while we were in St. Louis. I asked her what she had done with the corrugated iron."

"Did you not order it to be sold and taken away?"

"Who took it?"

"Really, Sister, I did not ask his name. He said you told him to sell it which he succeeded in doing."

Sister Blandina sensed trouble. "I saw we had been over-reached." She went to visit to the railroad freight agent and asked, "Have you had any heavy freighting lately?"

"The heaviest from Santa Fe was your corrugated iron assigned to Colonel Carpenter at Los Cerrillos. I hope [he] paid you a good price for it, because it was just what the Colonel wanted for his smelter." So now she knew who shipped the iron down to the mining town. The pieces of the puzzle were coming together.

The gentleman in question ran a planing mill and advertised his finished lumber products for sale in Santa Fe. She decided to order some doors and sashes from him. "The order was delivered quickly and in good condition. I gave a second order that likewise was filled promptly and satisfactorily. For the first order I mailed a check by return mail."

After the second order was filled, she sent him this message: "There are forty dollars due you; this being the difference between your bill and the

Photograph of San Francisco Street in 1880. Although not clearly visible, the cathedral was under construction at the end of the street. *Courtesy of the Palace of the Governors Photo Archives (NMHM/DCA) negative 052869.*

price of the corrugated iron, which you sold. Shall we mail you a check for the amount or will you be in town soon?" He soon turned up at her door. He professed confusion about her note regarding the forty dollars and asked for clarification.

"Forty dollars is the difference between the last order we gave you, and the price of the corrugated iron which you sold."

Feigning ignorance, he replied: "What has corrugated iron to do with your order to my mill?"

"Only this. When you pay for the iron which belonged to us, we shall pay your bill."

"I see, Sister, you compel me to resort to law to have you pay me what you owe me."

"Suit yourself," she replied. She expected to hear further from him about the predicament, but she was quite taken aback by what happened three days later.

"Are you Sister Blandina?" the lady asked.

"I am."

"Is it possible you are trying to ruin my husband and family by claiming money not owed you?"

"I trust not."

"My husband tells me you claim money for a sale of which he knows nothing. Sister, I cannot imagine a Sister of Charity trying financially to ruin a family. My husband put forth every effort to establish a mill for the benefit of the Territory. Now that he is established, you claim money not owed you."

"Suppose you let your husband and myself settle this business. I would suggest that you do not make this public—unless your husband tells you to."

"I will make it public. I will not see my husband and family ruined because you claim money not due you. I am going now to your own lawyer and expose you."

"Let me beg of you to permit this affair to be settled between us without any publicity…this I ask for the sake of yourself and family."

In a huff, the lady reiterated her threat to go immediately to the lawyer, turned and headed for the door. As she turned, Sister Blandina, spoke. "I will speak more clearly if you will calm yourself."

"I am as calm as a wife can be when she sees her husband and children on the brink of ruin and that by a Sister of Charity."

"Will you return to your home and deliver to your husband a message from me which I believe will settle our differences?"

"I will be glad to deliver your message."

Sister quickly jotted a note and handed it to the frustrated woman. It read: "I had hoped this affair would be settled without anyone's intervention. You are the consignee of our corrugated iron to Colonel Carpenter at Los Cerrillos. Mr. Conant, the freight agent, has your signature. I did my best to save your reputation and have you retain the love and respect of your wife and children; which to hold or lose is in your hands." She signed the note: "Yours to rehabilitate and not destroy." Three days later, the man came to give her the money for the corrugated iron!

7
Train Heaven

The irregularity of the trains is enough to aggravate the people, and make them curse the lack of mail facilities in the Territory. But when the train does come through without mail the English language, forcible in the extreme, cannot express the amount of vexation occasioned.
—*The* Santa Fe New Mexican, *December 7, 1880*

The novelty of train service from Santa Fe to the East was fast turning into routine only after a month of its inaugural arrival. The Atchison, Topeka & Santa Fe was trumpeting the achievement all over the country, and trains in and out of the city were loaded with people and goods. People were coming to explore this new land that became so accessible overnight, and New Mexicans were going east on the "fast" train to merchandise havens in Kansas City, St. Louis, Chicago and Atlantic Seaboard cities.

The AT&SF put on a special train to fete Santa Fe city officials on a complimentary sightseeing trip to Kansas. While they were reveling in their travel, improvements at the Santa Fe depot continued. A roundhouse, a sixty-foot wind tower and a fifteen-foot water tank were being installed.

Going south, the tracks headed straight for Albuquerque. To do so, the tracks headed into Pueblo tribal lands. The Pueblo tribes, more open to newcomers than the nomadic tribes of the prairies and mountains, would bear the brunt of the iron road. For it was not just a set of rails glistening in the desert sun, it was a pathway for invasion. Invasions of people, yes, but other invasions as well, just as Sister Blandina witnessed at her hospital.

Contagious diseases—smallpox and tuberculosis—followed the tracks and spread rapidly, brought by railroad work crews, tramps and health seekers. New insects, such as tent caterpillars, codling moths and peach tree borers, also rode the rails.

For the Native Americans, it was a movement they could only watch in bewilderment. Many Anglo leaders expected the Indians to be involved in the westward rail march. Archbishop Lamy, who welcomed the train as an opening of New Mexico to the world, urged the company to employ Native Americans: "Let them bring their wages to their families and let them secure the necessities of life and honest comforts to which a family have a right." Unfortunately, his plea was not heeded.

The first pueblo to suffer from the onslaught was the one just south of Santa Fe, Cochiti. As the tracks moved south, the construction workers dumped so much dirt and rocks into the pueblo's main irrigation ditch, the *acequia madre*, that the Indians could not grow their crops. The railroads were, naturally, built along level routes, and this required confiscation of arable, irrigable pueblo land where vegetable crops were cultivated.

The next pueblo to feel the weight of steel was Santo Domingo. No other tribe was more welcoming than this one when General Stephen Watts Kearny of the U.S. Army came to claim the land for America in 1846. From all accounts, Santo Domingo received the American forces with friendship and hospitality. They volunteered to be spies on the Mexican government, as scouts for the Army as it moved through the territory and as entertainers in the art of horsemanship. They were anxious to show the Americans that they could be useful in war against the Mexicans, Navajos or other marauding Indians.

The invading railroad smashed through their pastures, farmland, and ditches and passed within two hundred yards of the main village. In effect, it pillaged the tribe's land grant without advance notice or negotiation, nor did it offer to lease, gain permission or offer to purchase a right-of-way. And how could a small Indian tribe halt the advance of a 400,000-pound steam locomotive?

And the trains would not just be passing through. The railway created a permanent town only about two miles north of the Santo Domingo village. They named it Wallace, after Governor Wallace. The behemoth engines needed refueling stops about every one hundred miles, and this would become a permanent settlement to maintain the trains at the halfway mark between Las Vegas and Albuquerque. The newly created town would end up with several hundred residents, all workers for the railroad. A large stone roundhouse was erected, along with a restaurant and hotel, twelve houses and twenty-seven stores where whiskey was for sale.

The village became a magnet for local Indians who sat around the depot and occasionally picked up odd jobs carrying slop or washing dishes at the railroad establishments. Their farming jobs took a back seat, and the pueblo began a slow decline. Tribal elders complained bitterly to the local Indian agent, who could do nothing for them except send their complaints to the federal government.

One night, the train hit five bulls, two horses and two cows. Their owners found the animals lying dead around the track or so mangled that they had to be killed. It was to become a common event.

As a result of completed tracks to Santa Fe, the city replaced Las Vegas as the new terminus for stagecoach lines to carry travelers onward toward the west. The Southern Overland Mail coaches to Tucson, via La Mesilla and Silver City, offered passage for $98.25. New luxurious Concord coaches were put into service from La Mesilla to cities west. The Star Line now offered stage service from Santa Fe to Prescott for only $75.

Street scene, Cochiti Pueblo, first pueblo to be affected by the arrival of the railroad. *Created by T. Harmon Parkhurst; courtesy of the Palace of the Governors Photo Archives (NMHM/DCA) negative 002503.*

Santa Fe 1880

Wagons crossing railroad tracks at Santo Domingo Pueblo, site of Wallace, a town created by the railroad. *Created by John K. Hillers; courtesy of the Palace of the Governors Photo Archives (NMHM/DCA) negative 004359.*

Stories about visitor travelers coming into to town circulated and appeared in the newspaper. A Mr. Robinson from Missouri arrived in town with "a gold-handled cane and a Prince Albert hat." He had a wife and two children back home. He was attracted to the Mitchell Dramatic Company, which was about to present its third show, *Leah, the Forsaken.* He was hired to be the troupe's advance agent but in the process became involved with two of the women. The newspaper said he "borrowed $200" from one and eloped with the other! The owner of the drama company promptly fired him.

Two arguing men arrived at the depot in the middle of a ruckus. It seems they argued for days about a train car window as they traveled west. Reportedly one would say, "Shut that window." The other would reply, "Shut your mouth!" They were James Radliffe and John Roman, both citizens of Evansville, Indiana. Upon alighting in Santa Fe, Radliffe told the sheriff that the man following him was after his money. The sheriff put Roman in jail until midnight and then let him go.

The city hotels were having difficulty accommodating all the newcomers. The two main ones, Herlows's and the Exchange, lacked the upgrading needed to cope with newcomers who demanded not only a room but also proper service.

The *Santa Fe New Mexican* editor demanded, "More hotels are needed!" He reported that fourteen people, "well dressed ladies and gentlemen, were driven to both major hotels but there were no rooms. They returned to the depot, set up headquarters in a train car, ordered food from a restaurant then returned to the east!" The editor claimed, "It is easier to get fifty cents for a Mexican half dollar than to rent a room in Santa Fe!"

The Exchange was run-down and dilapidated. Six merchants in town, realizing its importance to the city, began fundraising to restore the old place. A total of $28,700 was pledged. A second story was planned to add more rooms, the dining hall would be enlarged and several retail shops and a barbershop opened.

People staying at the hotels had the option of enjoying the warm showers at Esselbach's Bath House downtown on West San Francisco Street. It offered hot and cold showers and was open from 7:00 to 9:00 a.m. It was near two other popular establishments: Gold's Provision House and the New Era Restaurant and Bakery.

A local hero was about to ride the train. In mid-January, Apaches in the San Marcos Mountains killed Lieutenant Harold French. His body was transported by wagon to Santa Fe and finally arrived a month later. The young, likeable officer was a favorite in the capital, and the city turned out to give him a fond farewell. He was taken in procession to the train depot. The newspaper said it was the largest funeral cortege in the city's history. He would now travel all the way to his family in Philadelphia. Six wounded soldiers would accompany him part of the way.

Chief Vitorio was again having success in marauding and terrorizing the south. His ability to elude troops sent to subdue him attracted new recruits to his cause, mainly from the Mescalero Apache Reservation. It was believed that the Mescaleros were not only joining but also feeding and arming the renegades. General Hatch was determined to end the Vitorio menace. He declared he would now march on the reservation and disarm and dismount the Indians.

In late February, he formed all the troops at his disposal into three battalions under Captains Morrow, Hooker and Carrol. He would use his three-pronged attack by approaching the San Andres Mountains from the east, north and west. Once Vitorio was defeated, he would tend to the troublesome Apache reservation. Soon, skirmishes took place nearly every day, but the biggest enemy was lack of water.

Major Morrow's command became exhausted after so many months chasing Vitorio. Morrow himself became ill, physically and emotionally.

> *I am heartily sick of this business and am convinced that the most expeditious and least expensive way to settle the Indian troubles in this section is to employ about 150 Apache Indian scouts and turn them loose on Vitorio without interference of troops...I have had eight engagements with the Vitorio Indians in the mountains since their return from Mexico and in each have driven and beaten them but there is no appreciable advantage gained, they run but make a stand at another point.*

Nevertheless, he vowed to continue. "I leave here tomorrow and will stick to Vitorio's trail so long as a serviceable animal or an able soldier is left but I still think that the pursuit is an unprofitable one." The next chase would take place in the Black Mountains and later east of the Rio Grande. Then Vitorio crossed the river and took refuge in the San Andres Mountains.

Meanwhile, Brigadier General John Pope, commander of the Army's Department of Missouri, conceived a plan to end the war. He obtained a commitment from the Department of Texas to send elements of the Tenth Army into New Mexico to assist. Colonel Benjamin Grierson was ordered to bring a detachment from Texas in April; their first objective would be to disarm and dismount the Mescaleros at their reservation.

Indian matters were also threatening from another direction: the north. The Utes, under the leadership of Chief Douglas, were relocated to a new reservation in the San Juan River basin of southern Colorado. The newspaper claimed the settlers in the area were not consulted on this new arrangement and called the Indians "worthless paupers who declare they will not work and who are a nuisance to any community." In late February, Douglas was also put on the train for Fort Leavenworth Prison. He attempted an escape but was quickly captured.

The Southern Utes, under a young leader, Ignacio, were threatening settlers at Tierra Amarillo and Chama in New Mexico. In the editor's opinion, the government should ship them East "and let them stretch their teepees on the beautiful lawns, arbors and front yards of the costly mansions of sympathizers."

At the hospital, Sister Blandina was called to help a lost soul who had come west on the train. His name was Joseph, but everyone just called him

Joe. "Do you know that Joe dances to the moon?" a patient asked the Sister. "I do not know that he dances at all," she replied.

"At about 10 o'clock p.m., Joe will go to the convalescents' adobe roof and dance as queer a death dance as any Apache can do," the patient responded in a mysterious whisper.

The next night when all was quiet and most in the hospital were asleep, a bell rang and Sister Blandina heard "intermingled with the sounds of the bell were groans, and occasionally the word 'Sister' could be distinguished. Five of us dovetailed in a room 15 by 15 feet. I noticed all had heard the bell and groans. I prepared to meet the trouble."

Sister Catherine's gentle voice whispered, "Sister Blandina, that is our Joe. I am going out to see what is the matter."

Noticing that the Sister was hesitating, not making a move, Sister Blandina decided to take the situation in hand: "I went where Joseph stood ringing the bell and groaning and asked: 'What is it, Joseph? Are you sick?'"

"Yes Sister, yes Sister. I am afraid."

"Sister Catherine and I will go with you to your room. You go in and go to bed, then we will come and pray…with you." He obeyed and the two Sisters followed and began praying. "The prayers calmed the worried mind. When we were ready to leave, he said: 'Sister, I must make a confession.'"

"Shall we go for the priest?"

"No, let me make it to you in Italian while I have the courage. What I did is so much on my mind that if I do not get it off I will go crazy." Then he shared with her the tale of his life, of misdeeds, of guilt, of regrets. She quietly listened and folded his secrets away in that part of her brain where confidential matters were forgotten.

8
The Archbishop Recovers

Shooting a man is becoming too monotonous for the Santa Fe roughs, and they are beginning to believe that to club the victim over the head with a pistol butt is preferable as it leaves a chance for further recreation.
—*The* Santa Fe New Mexican, *February 7, 1880*

When Sister Blandina stopped in one day in mid-March to check on the archbishop, she found him unusually alert. After more than two months confined to his bed, this morning he was sitting in his office actively discussing some aspect of the cathedral construction with several of the workmen. As she waited to have a word, she wandered to an adjoining room into his library, the finest in the territory.

Her hand brushed the cover of many well-worn and weathered volumes, theological works in Spanish, Latin, and French, published in the previous two centuries. Some were originally bound in leather and gold. There was a seven-volume collection of *Mystica Ciudad de Dios*, the "Divine History of the Virgin Mother of Christ," by Spanish nun Maria de Agreda. It was claimed that in the 1620s the nun appeared to numerous Indians in the Southwest while physically still in Spain; she introduced them to the cross. She was Mother Superior of the Discalced Sisters of St. Francis at Agreda, Spain. The faithful marveled at her bilocation ability to be in two places at once!

Among other books were volumes in Latin of Thomas Aquinas, a commentary on the Duodecim Prophets from Venice, a *Virgini Deiparae* from

Rome, a *Theologia Moralis* from Venice and a commentary on Proverbs from Brussels. Many of the books showed evidence of water damage.

They were obviously part of the priest's baggage when his ship went down some thirty years before in the Gulf of Mexico. It was on his maiden voyage to the Southwest, when he left his parish in Ohio and traveled by boat down the Ohio and Mississippi Rivers, then by ship from New Orleans to the Texas coast. Upon arrival at Matagordo Bay, the ship sank within sight of land and all aboard had to swim to shore. Fortunately, he was able to rescue most of his baggage. The final stages of his trip to Santa Fe were by donkey and cart to San Antonio and then across the desert into New Mexico. Many of the books in his library were survivors of that saltwater baptism.

She remembered listening intently years before when he told the Sisters of his "solitary journey to Durango, in 1851 where he verified his credentials as the new appointed bishop of Santa Fe with the Bishop of Durango. She thrilled to the Archbishop's account of his journey across the plains in 1867. Some of her own Sisters of Charity and Sisters of Loretto were with him back then when Indians attacked them.

"From his lips she heard of the bravery of Sister Augustine Barron, Sister of Charity, who forgot her own safety and went to the aid of a young man, the Bishop's Major Domo, who was dying of cholera during the Indian attack. During that same Indian attack, Archbishop Lamy told them, a very young Loretto Sister, Sister Alphonsa Thompson, died and was buried out there on the plains. Her grave has never been found."

Sister Blandina continued her reminisces as she gazed at the ancient books in the library. She "loved the legend of the famed statue of Our Lady, La Conquistadora," first brought to Santa Fe in 1598. When the Pueblo Indians revolted in 1680, she was taken to Texas for safety and returned with General De Vargas in 1692, when he retook the City of Holy Faith.

Sister Blandina contemplated the life of this extraordinary man, the archbishop. His travels amounted to thousands of miles and he still had more to go, assuming his health was, indeed, on the mend. His contributions to Santa Fe were prodigious. Schools, the hospital and the cathedral that was nearing completion all bore his mark. Ah, the cathedral! He brought with him the Romanesque style, with its Moorish echoes, that he inherited from his homeland of France. His mark on the city would be felt for centuries to come, she was sure. If only she could leave such a legacy.

Now he was beginning to feel his oats again, much to her relief. Though "scarcely able to write, having been ill for five weeks," he wrote to church officials in Europe: "Thanks to God I am still here." And his attention turned once again to the great cathedral's construction.

Built on a slight rise at the east end of town, it already dominated the city skyline. It was being built around the older adobe church that still stood—that church was left standing inside the new cathedral so that services could continue during the construction period. Groundbreaking for the new edifice took place back in 1869; the cornerstone laid by the archbishop himself. It was promptly stolen a week later and had to be replaced. Now, finally, the two corner towers at the front of the building were rising. He was anxious to see the work continue apace; he longed to see it completed.

Perhaps its prominence at the end of San Francisco Street was prompting optimism for new construction all around town. As the archbishop and the Sister sat for a few moments, they shared their concerns about what was happening in their city. With the arrival of the railroad, both were aware of the challenges to the church in meeting the rapidly changing scene.

The sell-out crowds at the Mitchell Dramatic Company performances at the makeshift Motley's Theater raised hopes by locals that a legitimate theater could be successful. Their most recent productions were *Divorce* and *The Lady of Lyon*.

Indeed, Dr. D.W. Mitchell, manager of the drama company, was in town "surveying the whole field." He declared that the city needed and could support a new theater. Stocks were now on sale for potential shareholders and $50,000 was already raised, according to the *Santa Fe New Mexican*. The money was given in cash; two burros were required to carry it, and three men were hired to guard it!

A new hotel, Miller's, was soon to be built. It would be a first-class accommodation located on the south side of the river. The San Francisco Street area was booming with commercial enterprise: the Senate Saloon, Hayt and Joy's Bookstore, Gold's Provisions, Esselbach's Baths, Lad's City Market and Club 34, among others.

Sister Blandina expressed her alarm at all the human suffering that city growth was causing. A serious railroad accident at a place called Coleman's Camp just outside of town was a good example. A locomotive was pushing a car piled high with railroad ties with workmen sitting on top, when the men saw a cow crossing the track. They foresaw an accident in the making and jumped off the train. The car then tipped over, and the ties fell on them. One of the workmen, M. Kingsley, was killed, and ten others were wounded.

One night in mid-March, an elderly lady was found dead in an alley off San Francisco Street. A man by the name of Pais was suspected of the crime

Right: St. Francis Cathedral under construction, 1880. Note the towers of the older church that was left standing inside, surrounded by the walls of the cathedral. *Photograph by Bennett and Brown; courtesy of the Palace of the Governors Photo Archives (NMHM/DCA) negative 127377.*

Below: Archbishop J.B. Lamy, second from left, and J.P. Machebeuf, third from right, in the archbishop's Santa Fe garden, 1880. *Courtesy of the Palace of the Governors Photo Archives (NMHM/DCA) negative 049017.*

and put in jail. The next day, he was taken from the jail by armed men and now was missing. Conjecture was that he was lynched.

Another two characters, James King and Charley Rice, were "overcome by the rosey," according to a recent edition of the *Santa Fe New Mexican*. They were found drunk in the gutter at night and taken to the jail. The next day, the jailer, Silva, permitted the prisoners to walk outside with their leg irons on, to bring in wood from the front of the jail. He then read one of Gough's temperance lectures and released them.

The newspaper reported that Susan Wallace, now writing in Indiana, described to one eastern newspaper a street scene in Santa Fe. She said most of the people she met in the city streets had Indian blood in their veins: "Perfectio, a worthless peon in a Navajo blanket sweeps the sidewalk; Benito, a shambling Mexican boy, watches his chance for a spring at the spoons, brings the daily mail; Mariposa, the silliest of slowboys pushes, pushes the baby wagon while Angelius, an angel whose form has lost its original brightness, lazily watches her."

Both the priest and the Sister were thankful that law and order, for the most part, prevailed in Santa Fe, as opposed to Las Vegas just forty miles to the east. There, it seemed, robbers and murderers ruled the town. The Dodge City Gang, that band of unsavory characters, was continuing its violent behavior. Their reputation as desperados in the cow towns of western Kansas followed them to New Mexico, but here they found fertile ground to accomplish their intrigues.

Remarkably, several members of the gang managed to obtain law enforcement jobs in Las Vegas! Hyman G. Neill, better know as "Hoodoo Brown," was appointed justice of the peace. He then recruited some of his old cohorts as law enforcement officers. With the criminal cartel all back together, they proceeded to continue their thieving bent. They held up two stagecoaches and two trains headed for Santa Fe. Now Federal Marshal John Sherman issued a warrant for Hoodoo Brown. The state government offered a $300 reward for anyone who could bring him to face justice in Santa Fe.

Meanwhile, an otherworldly event was witnessed at the train station at Galisteo Junction. Several people reported that a balloon of monstrous size was visible overhead. It was fish-shaped and propelled by a fan. Ten people onboard seemed to be having a party; their language was not understandable. It then suddenly ascended higher and headed east. The *Santa Fe New Mexican* speculated that it must have been an airship from Asia.

A silk flower and a cup had been thrown overboard and claimed by those on the ground who witnessed the bizarre event. The newspaper reported the cup to be of peculiar workmanship, entirely different to anything used in the United States. The flower was made with silk-like paper with characters that reminded the witnesses of designs they had seen on Japanese tea chests. The items were then put on display at the station. A week later, the newspaper reported the mystery solved: the balloon, or "Aerial Monster," was perhaps the first of a regular line of airships from China to America.

    Back in the archbishop's office, Sister Blandina noticed her chatter of city happenings was falling on deaf ears. She was remarking on the miracle of a new circular staircase in the Loretto Chapel, recently built by an unknown carpenter, when she noticed the archbishop was having difficulty attuning to her voice. His head nodded, and his eyes closed frequently. Finally, he dropped off to sleep sitting in his chair. She got up and headed for the door, which she closed ever so quietly.

9
The Governor Writes a Book

Young men don't swear. There is no occasion of swearing outside a newspaper office where it is useful in proofreading and indispensibly necessary in getting forms to press. It has been known also to materially assist an editor in looking over the paper after it is printed. But otherwise it is a very foolish habit.
—*The* Santa Fe New Mexican, *August 2, 1880*

Casual observers of officialdom in Santa Fe probably would never have guessed it, but the territorial governor, Lew Wallace, had a secret hobby that sustained him during the turbulent days of the booming capital city and the territory. During the day, he was a dutiful official tending to Indian Wars, military matters, the Lincoln County War and daily duties of his office. But at night, he was a recluse. He hid in a small room of the Palace of the Governors to take up his pen and write.

His evenings in a little room next to his office became "a perfect retreat from the annoyances of daily life as they are spun for me by enemies, and friends who might as well be enemies," he said. "When I reach the words 'The End' how beautiful they will look to me!" he wrote his wife, Susan, back in Indiana. The book was seven years in the making, research taking the bulk of that time. But it was in that little dark room in the palace where his writing brilliance found light.

At last, in March, he completed the final draft of the manuscript, all written in purple ink to honor the Easter season. He was pleased with the results, and now he could plan to take it to the editor in New York. Halfway there, his wife would meet him and travel with him the rest of the way to the big city.

One day before he was to leave, Flora Spiegelberg happened to pass by his office. "I looked into the window and the Governor beckoned to me to come in. He said: 'I have just wrapped up my manuscript of Ben Hur to forward to my publishers. Do you think it is worth the expressage (expense)?'"

For a moment, she stared at him, then replied, "I will gladly pay half of the expressage if you agree to divide the royalties with me!"

"I will consider your offer," he chuckled.

"It has been said that the royalties from the book, the play and film amounted to nearly $3,000,000. In later years I often joked with him about my offer and how wise he was not to have accepted it," she recalled.

Before departing in early April, Wallace turned over his duties to territorial secretary William G. Ritch, who would be acting governor in his absence. In New York, the Wallaces presented the manuscript to Joseph Henry Harper, of Harper & Brothers. "This is the most beautiful manuscript that has ever come into this house," effused Harper. "A bold experiment to make Christ a hero that has been often tried and always failed."

While the governor was away, the story of the Apache Vitorio was still being written. He was determined to continue avenging his tribe's displacement from their native home. Former Apache Indian agent John Ayers testified to officials in Santa Fe that the government was at fault for the current Apache raids—they forced the Indians to move from their ancestral home in Hot Springs to what seemed a distant land space in the Arizona Territory. Vitorio repeatedly asked for permission to settle his clan at Hot Springs, but government bureaucracy fumbled his pleas repeatedly. Now the territory would pay the price.

The *Santa Fe New Mexican* was diligent in reporting the Indian Wars in the south. It reported in mid-March that Apaches from the Mescalero Apache Reservation killed a rancher, Manuel Sanchez, near Alamo Canyon but let his son go home to report his father's death. Two more men were killed near Palomas.

Shortly thereafter, there were Indian attacks at Tierra Blanca, near Las Cruces. The newspaper reported, "The country is full of Indians." The Round Mountain Stage station was raided and all their stock stampeded. As the military units chased after the marauders, they headed again for safety into the San Mateo Mountains. Fighting Apaches in their mountain hideouts was not to the liking of the Army's Navajo scouts so they decided to desert.

A gunfight between the two sides took place at Embreo Canyon in early April. Captain Carroll's contingent led the military's attack and discovered Chief Nano, not Vitorio, led the Indian band. He was ensconced elsewhere in the mountain range. The soldiers then went in search of Vitorio, traveling forty-two miles through the desert without water, a heroic feat. The Army received intelligence that said the Mescaleros seemed to be abandoning Vitorio to his fate.

A dispatch to the capital gave details of Captain Carroll's efforts. Early on the morning of April 8, reinforcements arrived at Hembrillo Canyon to the sound of heavy gunfire and found Carroll pinned down and virtually surrounded. With the added help, the newly inspired soldiers chased Vitorio's band, which had scattered and hid among the rocks. Carroll had eight men wounded, including himself, and twenty-five horses and mules killed. He estimated close to twenty Indians dead, but scouts in the area found only one dead warrior. General Hatch soon arrived and ordered the Army units to head east for the Mescalero Apache Reservation.

Back in Santa Fe, preparations were underway to prepare for the visit of another general, one of the most famous: Ulysses Grant, former general of the U.S. Army and former president. W.F. Saunders, a reporter for the *Santa Fe New Mexican*, was elected secretary of the planning committee. A newspaper editorial fussed about the town's condition and its readiness to receive such royalty. It said of the plaza, "The quantity of filth and fertilizing substances which overspread the Plaza grounds suggests that it could be changed into a cabbage garden!"

Grant had interests in a mining venture south of the capital. No doubt he was coming to check up on his investment. The mining center, Cerrillos, was a booming town and suffering some of the same growth ailments as the capital. It had grown to boast several hotels, as many saloons and 36 houses inhabited by 250 residents that were mostly men.

The male population tended to erupt into disagreements and drunken brawls on a regular basis. Sister Blandina recently took in a man by the name of Al Shoemaker who had been knifed two times by an attacker. He was now in her hospital with erysipelas caused by the wound. Others were not so fortunate to have a hospital bed.

"Of the male patients brought to the hospital, only one remains of whose care we are in doubt," she wrote her sister. "This patient was caught in a blast; one eye is entirely gone. Dr. Longwell thinks there is a possibility of retaining the sight of his other eye, but the patient would have to be under the care of an eye specialist."

Left: Sketch of General Ullyses S. Grant. *Clipart courtesy FCIT, https://etc.usf.edu/clipart.*

Below: The mining town of Cerrillos, south of Santa Fe, in the 1880s. *Photograph by J.R. Riddle; courtesy of the Palace of the Governors Photo Archives (NMHM/DCA) negative 076056.*

Her immediate thought was of the good care provided back in her hometown of Cincinnati. "I wrote Sister Gabriella in charge of the Good Samaritan…asking if she would admit Tom Gleason in hopes that he might retain the sight of one eye. The answer was prompt from her kind colleague: "Send him on, Sister Blandina. I understand you are doing your share. I must do mine."

The patient's work boss told his fellow laborers, "Tom is going to be sent to Cincinnati in hopes his one eye can be saved. Let us make a collection for him." Sister Blandina accepted the money, helped Tom secure it on his person and sent him east on the train to Cincinnati.

In the same letter to her own sister, she turned philosophical as she mused about another incident in late April: "The thing that puzzles me most is that they for whom we make the most sacrifices become the shrewdest in over-reaching us." She always tried to be careful in her dealings with strangers who came for aid, but occasionally when she was taken advantage of, she wondered anew at the audacity of human deceit. On this occasion, it involved a dying woman and her husband.

> *The latest that causes my wonder is this: A hasty message was brought me at 9:30 P.M. Her husband is on his way to the hospital. He is bringing his wife, who is in a dying condition. The high altitude has affected her heart.*
>
> *We managed to make place for her. She was carried in at 10:30 P.M., and passed away at 11:00 P.M. The husband was inconsolable. He has a sawmill near Glorieta and she did the cooking for the hands at work, which helped him to carry on the sawmill. He gave me a pathetic story of his troubles and wanted to know if we could not accept a note on thirty days' time for lumber which we still need for different purposes,*
>
> *"Whether you want the lumber or not, I'll be at the bank to pay the face value of the note," he said. "By doing me this favor, I can pay my men and save my mill."*

Seeing the man in his hour of extreme sadness, Sister Blandina's sympathy overwhelmed her.

> *After consultation, we thought no greater act of charity could be performed. He told me he was a church-going man, but none of his denomination lived in this part of the country.*
>
> *Being a church-going man had no effect on me, but having seen his wife die and buried, and knowing that every man who drifted this way and had no capital to rely on, would claim his money for work done, and would surely endanger his mill if hands were not paid, we treated him as we would wish to be treated ourselves.*

Soon, they got notice from the bank that the note was due, and they paid it. Unfortunately, thereafter, they had "no sight of the mill man, nor have we heard from him." She concluded: "I am beginning to learn that human nature, since Adam was too pliant, and Eve too curious—is a strong mixture of good and evil."

10
The Stolen Madonna

Go to either one of our hotels at ten in the evening and ask for a room—then consider if a good hotel could not pay in Santa Fe.
—*The* Santa Fe New Mexican, *February 29, 1880*

In Santa Fe, May is a propitious month, when winter is well forgotten and the strong westerly winds of spring begin to give way to sunny, warmer days leading into early summer. Not only does nature come alive, but people also feel optimistic again for the coming pleasant days when life is most normal. The biggest event of the month is the May Corpus Christi procession. For hundreds of years, it always began at the downtown Rosario Chapel.

The chapel contained a tiny statue of the Madonna, La Conquistadora, made of wood and plaster with painted face and dress. Every year, she joined the procession as the faithful marched through the streets to pause at each improvised shrine, of which there were many. Any shop owner, resident or landowner who wished the congregation to pray for him or her would create a stopping point on the property.

This year, the marchers paused for a rest stop in front of the home of merchant Willi Spiegelberg and his wife, Flora. They set the ornate platform conveying La Conquistadora down on the street while they recovered from the heat of the day. While they chatted and without their seeing, the youngest Spiegelberg child ran out of the house and quietly took the Madonna up in her arms and excitedly carried her to her bedroom inside the house.

Santa Fe 1880

Corpus Christi procession on San Francisco Street around 1880. *Photograph by William Henry Jackson; courtesy of the Palace of the Governors Photo Archives (NMHM/DCA) negative 049166.*

Presently, the bearers took up their burden and continued toward the cathedral. When they arrived at their destination, they discovered with dismay that the Madonna was no longer with them. With chagrin and a bit of fear, they reported the loss and began a frantic search by retracing their steps and inquiring of everyone along the way if they had seen her. There was no sign of her.

That evening, the girl's mother went into the five-year-old's room to kiss her good night and found the Madonna tucked lovingly next to her in the bed. In great embarrassment, Flora Spiegelberg hurried to the archbishop's

The Madonna, La Conquistadora, as she stands in the sanctuary chapel in the Cathedral Basilica of St. Frances of Assisi. *Photograph by Robert H. Martin; courtesy of the Palace of the Governors Photo Archives (NMHM/DCA) negative 041427.*

Willi Spiegelberg, mayor of Santa Fe in the early 1880s. *Courtesy of the Palace of the Governors Photo Archives (NMHM/DCA) negative 050486.*

residence with the doll. Sputtering with apologies, her explanations were met with roars of laughter from the archbishop. He then invited his relieved guest to have a glass of wine with him.

Nothing more was said of the incident, but some months later, a package came from Paris to the Spiegelbergs. In it was a beautifully dressed wax doll for their daughter. There was a note explaining that it was "to replace the little Madonna."

No doubt the archbishop was thankful that the incident involved the conscientious Spiegelbergs, or the outcome might have been different. The Jewish merchants were leading families, successful businessmen and always willing to serve and gift the community. This year, Willi Spiegelberg was elected mayor, and with his brother they committed to building a new hotel in the city; the need was acute. The *Santa Fe New Mexican* heralded the opening of the Grand Central Hotel, and it claimed a fourth hotel was in the planning stage.

The hotels were desperately needed as passenger trains were now regularly arriving daily from the east and south at 8:20 p.m. and departing at 8:00 the next morning. Each train disgorged tourists eagerly looking for mementos of their trip. Mexican jewelry and Indian pottery were the most popular items. Gold's provision store claimed to have the largest stock of Indian pottery in the world, advertising "Ancient pottery from the Grand Quivira, chief city of the seven lost pueblos of the Aztec race!"

To meet the needs of the increased consumer demand in the growing city, freight cars were now more frequent, bringing supplies and goods, as well as fruits and vegetables, from the East. With the replacement of the Old Santa Fe Trail by the faster trains, perishable food could arrive in tolerably good condition. The May 20 newspaper announced, "a car load of potatoes arrived yesterday, also strawberries."

A traveling western troupe, called Captain Jack's, took over the plaza. "According to an announcement," reported the newspaper, "Captain Jack marched into the center of the Plaza...and threw his Winchester to his

The Spiegelberg store on San Francisco Street around 1880. *Sketch by William G. Ritch; courtesy of the Palace of the Governors Photo Archives (NMHM/DCA) negative 010777.*

shoulder, letting the shots succeed each other like a fusillade from a Gatlin gun. A large crowd of people witnessed the exhibition," which included dances, songs and farces.

An early summer activity for the Indians was a rabbit hunt, one sport in which women could take part. It was turned into a game for the younger set. Susan Wallace had the opportunity to witness the game and left a fascinating description:

> *We saw a party…hunting rabbits with clubs which they throw, making a whirring sound like to boomerang of eastern savages.*
>
> *If in whirling his missile a warrior misses a rabbit, which is finally killed by a squaw, he is obliged by law or custom, which is equally strong, to change clothes with her, and the return to the pueblo…in that guise. He must also keep her in fresh meat during the next winter, serving out his term of degradation in feminine belongings, a target of…mirth, and, for the season, the village fool. Under such humiliating penalty for failure, we may imagine the experts throw the club with wondrous care and skill when women join in the chase.*

Horse races and cockfights were continuing to attract local crowds, Indians, Mexicans and Anglos. Mostly young Mexican and Indian horse riders played another gruesome game: Correr El Gado, or Chicken Race, usually organized on religious holidays. The *Santa Fe New Mexican* reported on June 28 that Abram Herrera and Anato Martinez won the game on St. John's Day at Agua Fria, a settlement just on the western side of Santa Fe.

Watched by the crowd, the boys rode burros and tried to grab the head of a chicken that has its body buried in the sand. The first one to accomplish the task was then chased by all the other contestants, who tried to wrest the bird from the rider. The one holding the bird when it died won the trophy At the hospital, Sister Blandina could expect casualties from the sport: horse kicks, chicken scratches and body blows.

And with the constant influx of visitors, the Sisters of Charity had to treat various new diseases that were showing up at the hospital. Consumption was the major complaint. Even so, Sister Blandina's diary noted only a singular incident in May: "Dr. Symington was angry with me for attending to a patient without my gloves."

He asked, "Do you not realize the danger you run?"

"Yes, Doctor, but I am not afraid."

He countered, "And the disease is not afraid of you."

Apparently, the decomposed body of a man had been found and needed attending to. Sister Blandina and a helper named Joseph made the coffin, "but when we were ready to place him in, piece by piece, every convalescent patient disappeared, including our Joseph. So piece-by-piece I placed the corrupted body in the coffin. The stench made me think of the descriptions of the lower regions given by Dante in his Inferno. I was just putting the lid on the coffin when our Joseph came to the mortuary room door. The expression on his face showed his fear of infection and shame at having left me alone. Though Dr. Symington professes no religion, I believe he was much disturbed because I gave so much time to this Lutheran patient."

With the influx of people of all types into the city, she was encountering more and more people of different religions. Early on, she had met Mormons and Methodists. Presbyterians were well established with a church, and an Episcopal church was soon to be built, known as the Church of Holy Faith. Missionaries from various faiths were busy distributing tracts and Bibles. She muttered, "A man is a man for all that," as she laid the Lutheran body in a grave.

Republican senators in the U.S. Congress were able to get a Homestead Bill passed that summer, and the act was sure to add more to the migration of people from the East to the Southwest. Gold, silver, copper and turquoise mines called the Cerrillos, Old Placer, New Placer and Silver Butte beckoned prospectors to the Southwest.

By June, the *Santa Fe New Mexican* boasted that Santa Fe had the largest population of any city in New Mexico, about six thousand, and more business interests than any city in either New Mexico or Colorado. Stores were beginning to install show windows filled with merchandise from around the world. It was not uncommon to see advertisements touting apparel from New York, Chicago or even London and Paris.

New Mexico itself was adding items to local markets; corn, wheat, oats and vegetables were grown locally. Ranches were supplying meat and poultry, and even cotton was being grown where ancient water acequias made irrigation possible. The newspaper carried an article from the *New York Times* that lauded New Mexico agriculture but noted the "lawlessness of the population."

Even people in Santa Fe had to agree that lawlessness was a major danger to people coming west, and it contributed to fears that the burgeoning growth could falter if gunslingers and Indians could not be brought under control. The coming months would reveal whether or not there could be improvements in that direction.

Santa Fe 1880

While the city frolicked in the good June weather—the temperatures rarely rose above ninety under clear blue skies—a major concern of the territorial government continued to be happenings in the south. Indian raids and gun battles in Lincoln County continued to steal the newspaper headlines.

11
Closing in on Vitorio

Tombstone is to have two new papers, one of which is the Tombstone Epitaph. The editor will doubtless have an affinity for "the devil," and "dead matter" and will be the right sort of man to "kill" spring poetry.
—*The* Santa Fe New Mexican, *April 19, 1880*

While Santa Fe basked in the sunshine of early summer, General Hatch and his buffalo soldiers were ranging along the Rio Grande trying to track down Vitorio. And from the east, Captain Grierson was leading an Army contingent into New Mexico from the Texas border. In the eastern mountains, he rounded up several small parties of Mescaleros and drove them back to their reservation. Then he hastened to meet up with the troops along the Rio Grande.

Meanwhile, Vitorio was also on the move and by mid-May had crossed the great river into the Mongollon Mountains. On the way, he killed sheepherders and anyone else who crossed his path. Among the slain was a miner, James C. Cooney, brother of Captain Cooney, commander of A Company, 9th Cavalry, and well known back in Santa Fe. Sadly, he had the task of personally burying his brother.

News of Vitorio's whereabouts came to the Barlo and Sanders Stage Stop near Tularosa. According to Army records, "Sergeant George Jordan and a detachment of 25 soldiers were at the station and preparing to call it a night. Upon the news, they saddled their horses and marched through the night and arrived at Old Fort Tularosa early the next morning." The troopers set to work building a stockade; local residents entered the stockade for safety, and the fast work of the soldiers saved the day. That evening, the Apaches attacked but were fought off by the soldiers' gunfire.

With this defeat, it was reported that Vitorio headed west in the direction of Mexico. In early June, Morrow intercepted an Indian party in his area headed in that direction. They pursued the Indian party and ended up killing two and wounding three others. They were surprised to discover one of those they killed was Vitorio's own son. The rest were riding fast toward the Mexican border.

A frustrated General Hatch telegraphed headquarters to see if something could be done to permit the American army to pursue the renegades into Mexico. Ten days later, the reply came that the Mexican government refused to permit American troops to enter its territory. Nevertheless, near the border, Hatch came upon a war party at the headwaters of the Palomas River, and his troops killed thirty Indians and counted some Navajo and Comanche among the dead.

For his failure to eliminate the Indian menace, a newspaper editor in the south called for Hatch's resignation. The newspaper claimed that Hatch was "a notorious liar" and asserted he "paid" to keep the Indian Wars in New Mexico. It pointed to the loss of soldiers and the general's failure to catch the culprits as reasons for him to resign.

Complaints about Hatch reached the capital, where, in early July, his superior, General Pope, arrived to consult with Governor Wallace, who was now back from his trip to New York. Rumors were flying that the general, who was even now chasing the Apaches, would be replaced. The editor of the *Santa Fe New Mexican* threatened "the territorial press will pour wrath upon the governor if Hatch is replaced."

While the Army was busy in the south, life continued to be wild in other parts of the territory. The governor, back in his office, was still monitoring the Lincoln County situation and alarming events in Las Vegas, the wild town east of Santa Fe. There, one Dr. John Henry Holliday was part owner of a downtown saloon that made him a wealthy man, but it became known for its rowdy gunfights. Holliday was born in Griffin, Georgia, but drifted west to the drier climate when he contracted tuberculosis.

He studied dentistry in his early twenties and practiced the profession whenever in need of funds; he became known as "Doc Holliday." The rest of the time, he was a gunman with a deadly aim. He drew his six guns with dedicated calm. Rumors about his ability as a sharpshooter seemed to outweigh actual reality. Holliday found he was most comfortable in dance halls, saloons and bordellos. He was an inveterate gambler and often acted as an in-house cardsharp. He was wiry and strong and often doubled as a resident gunman and bouncer. He knew his cards and enticed people to his table to play with him; he always won.

An incident in June 1880 was typical of his escapades. He entered a saloon in Las Vegas and got into an argument with bartender Charley White. Holliday had run the man out of Dodge City months before. The argument ended up with both men drawing their guns and, as usual, Doc's was the better aim. White fell when he got hit by Doc's lead bullet and collapsed behind the bar. Doc went on his way, thinking he had done his deadly duty. Next day, much to his surprise, he discovered that White had survived with only a slight wound.

It was said Doc had only one friend in the world: Wyatt Earp, the sheriff at Dodge City, Kansas. Earp found that Doc always had his back. It became well known that anyone picking a fight with Earp was also picking a fight with Doc. Except for about three years when Doc was running his Las Vegas saloon, the two men were inseparable, supporting each other with lies if need be. Their biggest showdown would come in 1881 when they traveled through Santa Fe on their way to Tombstone, Arizona, where they had a shoot-out at the OK Corral.

A woman, Kate Fisher, caused the shoot-out between Earp and Holliday with the Clanton-McLowery group. Kate was a large woman, whose voice was heard loud and strident, mainly because she was drunk most of the time. She was a few inches taller than Doc and gained the nickname "Big Nosed Kate." In mid-1880, she followed him to Tombstone. Some months later, the two got into a drunken argument, and Doc threw her out of his room.

About this same time, there was a robbery of a Wells Fargo stagecoach near the town, and Kate, angry with Doc, claimed he had robbed the stagecoach and killed the driver. At the same time, she made friends with the Clanton brothers. Doc defended himself to the local sheriff, John Behan, and was supported by Earp, now Arizona's U.S. marshal. Doc then angrily told Kate never to speak to him again.

But Kate continued to stoke the rumor that Doc had done the robbery. Infuriated, he took his anger out on the Clanton-McLowery clan for supporting her claim—and maybe more, for stealing Kate from him. Doc then entered a saloon where Ike Clanton was drinking and cursed him loudly. Clanton, knowing how fast Doc was with a gun, begged to be spared. He was later pistol-whipped in the main street by Wyatt Earp.

As a result, the Clanton and McLowery brothers challenged the Earp bothers to a gun duel. In the shoot-out at the OK Corral, Tom McLowery was shot dead by Holliday, who was wounded in the side. The shoot-out was not the end of the story, but the feud finally died down when Wyatt decided to move his family to California. Doc preferred to stay in the rough-and-ready backwater towns of the west.

By 1880, most news was transmitted by telegraph, and the *Santa Fe New Mexican* relied on the service to fill its pages. But the editor frequently complained about the way the local Western Union telegraph office operated. He claimed, in the July 2 edition, that townspeople in Santa Fe did not have confidence in the telegraph office manager: "Important dispatches are frequently sent by mail to Las Vegas, thence to be forwarded over the line or by the military line to Denison, Texas, where they are handed over to the Western Union office there." The newspaper also noted that registered mail was being sent to Alamosa, Colorado, then by buckboard to Santa Fe.

In Santa Fe itself, a big event was overshadowing whatever news came in from the rest of the world: General Grant's arrival. For months, local committees had been at work making preparations. Now, he was in town being feted at every turn over the extended Fourth of July holiday. His first visit was to the mines south of town, in which he had personally invested. Then he returned to town to participate in several receptions.

"Long before the hour when the iron horse that drew the iron-hearted commander triumphantly into the city had arrived, thousands of people assembled at the depot to greet the incoming train," reported the *Santa Fe New Mexican*. When the general alighted from the train, a welcome speech was given by local city leader T.B. Catron. "This duty is peculiarly pleasant to us, from the fact that you are the first of all men who, having held the high office of chief executive of any nation, has ever set foot upon the soil of New Mexico," he said.

The general gave a brief response, and "the visitors were then shown to their carriages and conveyed to the plaza. General Grant rode in a carriage drawn by four white horses, and preceded by the band of the 13th Infantry." A reception and further celebrations continued at the Palace of the Governors.

The holiday was also celebrated at the little Sisters of Charity hospital. Sister Blandina attempted to explain to the orphan girls the "full importance of this day." While she was with the children, a messenger came to speak to her privately, and "the knowledge he imparted aged me ten years in a few minutes." The upsetting news, probably brought by an assistant to the archbishop, or even himself, informed her that there was a move to replace the Sisters of Charity in Santa Fe by another religious order.

"My answer was such a firm 'NO' that my allegiance to the rules and constitutions of the Sisters of Charity of Cincinnati, Ohio, cannot be called in question." The reasons given for the threatened change were: "You are so far from the Motherhouse, and the local Superior is restricted by rule in many ways; waiting answers to permissions asked is a slow process. Moreover, few understand the needs of our southwestern missions. Only those who are actively engaged in the work are fit judges."

She attempted to reason with the theologian, "The Jesuits are here and (in my estimation) they are one of the best organized and one of the best governed Orders in the Church. Their General resides in Rome; it is somewhat farther than Cincinnati."

He left her saying, "I will not take this as your final answer."

Indeed, the subject came up soon enough. Several weeks later, she was able to report the final decision: "The subject of establishing a new community has been threshed out with a number of our best theologians. The pivot upon which the new community relies is immovable…hence I predict there will be no new community." A few months later, the Sisters of Charity in Cincinnati sent five new Sisters to bolster the workforce.

12
A Flooded Desert

New Mexico is a territory and her sufferings and wrongs are passed by unnoticed, while her citizens die and her interests suffer by reason of the criminal neglect of her necessities from those in high power.
—*The* Santa Fe New Mexican, *May 10, 1880*

July in Santa Fe is usually one of the most pleasant times of year. Susan Wallace left this description of a July she experienced:

> It is the month of July and the cottonwood trees of the Plaza are a mass of tender leafage in restless flutter, giving color and cool sound, most grateful in a land where sterility is the rule, fertility the rare and marked exception. The acequias are open, and they moisten earth and air in the square of alfalfa, or Spanish clover, knee-deep.

July 1880 began much as Susan described but the month ended up a disaster of unusual proportions. Rain started falling and continued to fall. Waterways flooded, making travel on the muddy roads difficult and causing disruptions to train and stagecoach services. On the first of August, four coaches arrived from Las Vegas two hours late because roads were almost impassable. The *Santa Fe New Mexican* reported the flood stage at eight feet in some places.

A train engineer on the AT&SF was killed and others injured because the rails spread when the train was traveling at moderate speed east of the

Acequia Madre irrigation ditch carried water through a large part of the city in 1880. A water distribution system was inaugurated a year later. *Courtesy of the Palace of the Governors Photo Archives (NMHM/DCA) negative 055021.*

Santa Fe 1880

Train on bridge in Apache Canyon that was washed out in the floods of summer, 1880. *Photograph by Bennett and Brown; courtesy of the Palace of the Governors Photo Archives (NMHM/DCA) negative 037441.*

city. The engine was thrown off the track into a ditch. Trains into Santa Fe were delayed until repairs could be made to the track. A bridge at Apache Canyon, just outside the city, was washed out and passengers had to be ferried into town by wagon.

Nevertheless, the burgeoning commerce in the city continued. General Grant's visit concluded early in the month but not before he was elected president of the San Pedro and Canyon del Agua Mining Company that touted capital of $10,000. Stocks in the company jumped from $2 to $375. Grant's salary was set at $25,000 per year. The operation included a six-thousand-acre property, and the mine reportedly had a thirty-foot vein of copper and gold.

Two significant ventures were also reported in the newspaper: a gasworks building was being constructed to bring street and domestic lighting to the city by the end of the year, and a water company was being formed to provide water distribution. It would require the construction of reservoirs in the Sangre de Cristo Mountains above town to catch and store the snowmelt waters of the Santa Fe River for domestic consumption. It would mean no more hauling water by hand from the river.

More notables were arriving in town. Ex-general Albert Pike was in town for a couple weeks, his intentions unknown but presumed to have something to do with mining. An imposing figure, Pike was six feet tall and weighed three hundred pounds. In earlier years, he had joined an expedition from St. Louis, Missouri, to Taos in New Mexico. He was also a legend from an early 1880s trapping expedition to the Llano Estacado, the vast plains of eastern New Mexico and northwest Texas.

It was announced that President Hayes, Secretary of War Ramsay and General Sherman would be visiting Santa Fe in October. Of much less notoriety and hardly noticed by locals, an archeologist by the name of Adolf Bandelier arrived in August. A leader in the comparative study of human societies, he was sponsored by the newly created Archaeological Institute of America. His exploration of native ruins in the Southwest would make his remembrance more enduring than all the other personages who arrived in the city this year.

From the now infamous Lincoln County in the south came news that confirmed the area as a war zone. During the recent Fourth of July celebrations, a drunken man by the name of Harriman was put in jail. Soon after, a mob got into the jail and, according to the newspaper, "riddled him with bullets." It also said the deputy sheriff was an accessory to the crime. The next day, a mob entered the jail and took another man out and hanged him.

When Sister Blandina heard the news, she no doubt remembered her intervention in a hanging, back in her Trinidad days. Back then, one of her older students, John, came to ask to have his sister excused from school. "He looked so deathly pale that I inquired, 'What has happened?' He answered, 'Haven't you heard?'

"Nothing that should make you look as you do," she replied.

"Sister, dad shot a man! He's in jail. A mob has gathered and placed men about forty feet apart from the jail to Mr. McCaferty's room. The instant he breathes his last, the signal of his death will be given, and the mob will go to the jail and drag dad out and hang him."

"Have you thought of anything that might save him?" she asked.

"Nothing, Sister; nothing can be done."

"Is there no hope that the wounded man may recover?" she implored.

"No hope whatever, the gun was loaded with tin shot," he replied.

Quickly, like lightening, a plan formed in her mind. "John, go to the jail and ask your father if he will take a chance at not being hanged by a mob."

"What do you propose doing, Sister?"

She quickly outlined her plan: "First to visit the wounded man and ask if he will receive your father and forgive him, with the understanding that the full force of the law be carried out."

John was quick to sense the danger, "Sister, the mob would tear him to pieces before he was ten feet from the jail."

"I believe he will not be touched if I accompany him," she said confidently.

"I'm afraid he will not have the courage to do as you propose," John rejoined.

She probably patted John on the back as she said, "That is the only thing I can see that will save him from the mob law. Ask your father to decide. This is Friday. I'll visit the sick man after school this afternoon. Let me know if he will consent to go with me to the sick man's room."

Immediately after school, she went with a companion to see the wounded man. Another nurse was already at the wounded man's side, writing his last letter to his mother "bidding her good-bye until they would meet where the Judge was just, and their tears would be dried forever.

"I looked at the young man, a fine specimen of honesty and manliness. My heart ached for the mother who expected frequent word from her son, then to receive such news! To be shot unjustly, to die in a strange land, among strangers, so young!"

Sister Blandina quietly explained her visit to the man in the bed. His reply was as she hoped: "I forgive him, as I hope to be forgiven, but I want the law to take its course."

She nodded her agreement, then asked: "Will you tell your assailant this if he comes to beg your pardon?"

"Yes, Sister," he replied.

That evening, John came to say his father was very much afraid to walk the short distance to McCaferty's room, "but if Sister would walk with him, he would take the chance of having the court pronounce sentence on him."

"Early Saturday morning we presented ourselves to the Sheriff in his office."

"Good morning, Sister!" was the sheriff's pleasant greeting.

"Good morning, Mr. Sheriff. Needless to ask if you know what is taking place…"

"You mean the men ready to lynch the prisoner who so unjustly shot the young Irishman?" said the sheriff with certainty.

Sister stood to her full height and with a voice of authority said, "What are you going to do to prevent the lynching?"

"Do! What has any sheriff here ever been able to do to prevent a mob from carrying out its intent?" he reacted by throwing out his arms in a helpless gesture.

"Be the first sheriff to make the attempt!" she replied indignantly.

"How, Sister?" He stood at his full height; she guessed he was six foot four. He impressed her as a person with "plenty of reserve strength."

She softly explained her plan: "The prisoner was asked if he would be willing to walk between the sheriff and Sister to the victim's sick bed and ask his pardon."

"Sister, have you ever seen the working of a mob?" he interrupted.

"A few, Mr. Sheriff."

"And would you take the chance of having the prisoner snatched from between us and hanged to the nearest cottonwood?"

"In my opinion, there is nothing to fear," she replied.

"If you are not afraid, neither am I." With that, the deal was done.

She described in her journal how it turned out:

> *We—the sheriff, my companion and myself—started to walk to the jail. All along the main street and leading to the jail were men at about a distance of a rod apart. These were the men who were to signal Mr. McCaferty's death by three taps of our school bell, in order that the mob might proceed to the jail, take the prisoner and hang him.*
>
> *Our group arrived at the jail, where we encountered the greatest discouragement. The prisoner saw us coming. When we got near enough to speak to him, he was trembling like an aspen. We saw his courage had failed him. We paused while we assured him he was safe in going with us.*
>
> *He hesitated, and then said, "I'll go with you."*
>
> *All along the road we kept silence, and no one spoke to us. When we got within a block of the sick man's room, we saw a crowd of men outside his*

Santa Fe 1880

door. It was at this juncture that my fears for the prisoner began. Intent upon saving our protégé from mob law, we hastened to the sick man's door. The crowd made way. Intense fear took possession of me.

The Sheriff and I remained at the foot of the few steps which led into the room...the door was left wide open that those standing outside might hear the conversation taking place within. The culprit stood before his victim with bowed head.

Fearing a prolonged silence, I addressed the prisoner: 'Have you nothing to say?'"

He lifted his head to look in the man's eyes and said, "My boy, I did not know what I was doing. Forgive me."

She went on to say:

The sick man removed the blanket which covered his tin-shot leg, revealing a sight to unnerve the stoutest heart. The whole leg was mortified and swollen out of proportion, showing where the poisonous tin had lodged and the mortification creeping toward the heart.

"I'm sorry, my boy, forgive me," said the man with tears in his eyes.

The reply was heartfelt: "I forgive you, as I hope to be forgiven, but the law must take its course."

Sister Blandina repeated the sentiment loud enough for all those gathered at the door to hear, "Yes, the law must take its course—not mob law."

Some days later, the circuit court came to Trinidad. It sentenced the prisoner to ten years in the penitentiary. McCaferty had lived three days after being shot, so the sentence was for manslaughter, not murder. Sister Blandina predicted the man would be out of jail in less than two years.

13
The Governor at Wit's End

The Utes get about $30 each from the government for signing the late treaty. Within two weeks after the money is received, it will be turned into Winchester rifles and ammunition and the red men will be better equipped for the spring campaign than the miners.
—*The* Santa Fe New Mexican, *December 7, 1880*

Governor Lew Wallace had seen a lot in life but nothing like the challenges he faced now in New Mexico. An experienced military man, at nineteen he was commissioned a second lieutenant in the U.S. Army during the Mexican-American War. He then became a first lieutenant during the American Civil War and fought at five famous battles, including the Battle of Shiloh in Tennessee. He served for a short time in the Mexican military a few years before President Hayes appointed him governor of the New Mexico Territory. He considered himself an honorable, trustworthy and capable leader. However, he often despaired for the territory: "Every calculation based on experience elsewhere, fails in New Mexico."

And now, here he was trying to tame an Indian chief who would not fit into any of the military roles Wallace had ever experienced before. In a sense, he admired the renegade: "In some respects he is a wonderful man, and, commencing with a band of seventy-five warriors, he succeeded in uniting tribes always hostile to one another before, and in a few weeks he had three hundred well-armed followers." The Apache warrior was pulling

Lew Wallace in his younger military years. *Courtesy of the Palace of the Governors Photo Archives (NMHM/DCA) negative 077788.*

in young braves from various tribes, those who were, like him, displaced socially and geographically.

For a military mind, it was difficult for the governor to understand how such an enemy could carry on a battle for so long—for a year now. He was constantly menacing the sparse populations in the large open spaces and mountains of the territory's south. The governor's resources were not sufficient to crush the rebellion: "The few men that I have can only check, but cannot crush him. Our officers and soldiers have displayed the utmost gallantry under the most discouraging circumstances."

The renegade was a brilliant strategist and well knew the governor's limitations, and he played them to his advantage. He not only knew that the governor's military resources were limited, but the vastness of the territory was also in his favor. To these advantages, add the well-known adaptation abilities of the Native Americans to the harsh conditions of the Southwest, their knowledge of the environment and their heritage of survival; these continued to make them a constantly vanishing prey. Vitorio was also aware of the various governments' sense of boundaries: New Mexico, Arizona, Texas and especially old Mexico all had defined frontier borders, and this gave him the advantage of stealthy escape.

Wallace related an incident that reveals the frustration he experienced during most of his term as governor.

> *I set out from Santa Fe to investigate difficulties in a remote region of the territory. I went in an ambulance, then the usual mode of travel, with a strong guard armed with Winchester rifles. After a few hours, Indians began to appear in the distance. My men held up their Winchesters, and the savages were careful not to approach within range.*
>
> *When we reached the town the people came out and greeted us with amazement; had we been newly raised from the dead, they could not have shown greater awe. We presently learned the cause. After returning the salutations of the officials, we followed them to the church. Before the altar were sixteen corpses, men women, children, some of them shockingly mutilated.*

So the government's battle with Vitorio's band was more than a cat-and-mouse game; it had turned into a death grip that only the strongest could win. Before the war was over, the governor would count over four hundred residents dead and more than an equal number of slain Native Americans.

In his latest escape, Vitorio, chased as never before by the buffalo soldiers, found sanctuary across the border in Mexico. Captain Grierson, traveling southward along the Rio Grande at the end of July, where summer temperatures ranged in the triple digits, arrived at the abandoned Fort Quitman on the Rio Grande in Texas. Much to his surprise, he discovered the troops of Mexican general Valle were encamped just across the river. They had skirmished with Vitorio on the Mexican side and were stalled at the riverside and badly in need of supplies.

Santa Fe 1880

The Americans shared their supplies with the tired Mexicans, while Vitorio circled south and slipped into Texas. News came by couriers that the Indian band had entered Texas at Eagle Pass. Grierson went in pursuit. He organized an ambush but was not successful in surprising the Indians, who headed, once again, toward the Rio Grande and into Mexico. It turned out to be Vitorio's last appearance on American soil.

Just when one Indian threat seemed to be resolved, another was threatening in the territory's north. The Ute tribe was up in arms over the encroachment of white settlements in southern Colorado. Their anger spilled over into New Mexico in the form of raids on border towns in the north. In early August, the *Santa Fe New Mexican* reported that a Ute Commission was in session at Los Pinos at the border amid demands by Coloradans that the Utes be moved out of their state. The *Santa Fe New Mexican* predicted the Indians would not want to leave their homeland in Colorado and would go on the warpath rather than move.

The issue was seemingly resolved on July 29 when forty-eight chiefs of the Utes signed a new treaty to give up their reservation in Colorado. Eventually, they would retain a few rights in Colorado, but some of the tribe would move westward into Utah Territory.

Governor Wallace also was concerned about Navajo raids in the west. The *Santa Fe New Mexican* reported raiders from that tribe were stealing horses and threatening the northwestern regions of New Mexico. In its August 2 edition, the newspaper announced no mail service was available westward from Fort Wingate, near the Arizona border.

But it was not only Indians that bedeviled the governor. The Lincoln County War seemed to never end. Billy the Kid became the symbol for all that was evil behind the continuing disturbances in the huge southern county. In 1879, Wallace agreed to a deal proffered by Billy the Kid: he would turn state's witness in the case of three accused murderers in exchange for a full pardon by the governor. Wallace said that if he surrendered and testified against the murderers, he would grant the pardon. But Billy said he did not like the idea of surrendering, it would appear as if he was a coward.

Wallace then suggested he could organize a fake arrest, one that would make it look like Billy had put up a fierce resistance. The fake arrest was made, and he testified in court against the killers. But Billy, once he found himself the center of attention, began to talk and would not shut up—he rambled on and on about all the outlaws in the territory, providing details about their thieving and cattle rustling, thus breaking the code of silence binding all criminals.

A second part of the bargain between Billy and the governor was that he would be tried for the murder of Lincoln County sheriff William J. Brady and two of his deputies in 1878. Wallace assured Billy that he would be set free after the trial, but the Kid grew uneasy waiting for the trial to begin and decided to skip town. In the process, he encountered the Texas gunman Joe Grant, who earlier let it be widely known that he would capture the Kid and claim a reward for his capture.

The two met and in a friendly gesture, Billy chatted with the gunman and admired his expensive six-shooter. The Texan foolishly handed the gun over for inspection to Billy, who proceeded to slyly turn the cylinder to three empty chambers. Billy handed back the gun, they squared off and fired at each other. Grant's gun clicked but failed to fire and Billy's shot rang true. Grant was dead, and the governor demanded Billy the Kid be caught and announced a reward for his capture.

When a posse surrounded Billy and his gang some weeks later at a ranch house, Billy hoisted a white flag for truce. When a member of the posse stepped forward to negotiate, Billy shot him dead. The rest of the men in the posse fled in terror. The Kid and his men rode away.

Things started to change when Pat Garrett, a former card-playing friend of Billy's, became sheriff of Lincoln County. The friendship changed when Garrett put on his sheriff's badge, and the governor again demanded capture of Billy the Kid. The summer of 1880 saw Billy on the loose, but his days of freedom were numbered.

As Sister Blandina heard the news from Lincoln County, she recalled her encounter with the famous gunman back in Trinidad. The episode started with an incident in the northwestern New Mexico town of Cimarron. One day, Sister Blandina happened to pick up an edition of the *Trinidad Enterprise*, where she read an exciting description of a gunman's antics that scared the people of Cimarron. He rode through town on his horse with his six-shooters held high yelling commands at the scattering citizenry.

Not long after, he appeared in Trinidad. "He was mounted on a spirited stallion and was dressed as the Toreadores (bullfighters) dress in old Mexico. Cowboy's sombrero, fantastically trimmed, red velvet knee breeches, green velvet short coat, long sharp spurs, gold and green saddle cover. A figure of six feet three, on a beautiful animal…the rider drew attention. The impression made on me was one of intense loathing, and I candidly acknowledge, of fear also." He then passed from her view.

Some weeks later, Sister Blandina was informed that the gunman she had seen got into an argument with his partner, Happy Jack, who drew his gun

Santa Fe 1880

The Lincoln County Courthouse where Billy the Kid made his last escape. *Courtesy of the Palace of the Governors Photo Archives (NMHM/DCA) negative 104821.*

first and now the man, Schneider was his name, was lying wounded in an abandoned adobe shed suffering from his wound. Always one to give aid where it was needed, Sister Blandina recorded what happened next: "At the noon hour we carried nourishing food, water, castile soap and linens to the sick and neglected man.

"I see that nothing but a bullet through your brain will finish you!" she chided him. "I saw a quivering smile pass over his face, and his tiger eyes gleamed. My words seemed heartless. I had gone to make up for the inhuman treatment given by others, and instead, I had added to the inhumanity by my words. After a few days of retrospection, I concluded it was not I who had spoken, but Fear, so psychologists say."

"What shall I call you?" Schneider asked.

"Sister," she said.

"Well, Sister, I am very glad you came to see me. Will you come again?"

She agreed to come to him on a daily basis and those days turned into weeks and the weeks into months. One day, as she was changing his bandages, he spoke tenderly of her first visit. "Had you spoken to me of repentance, honesty, morals or anything pertaining to religion, I would have ordered you out. 'I see that nothing but a bullet through your brain will finish you.' Sister, you have no idea what strength and courage those words put into me!"

He was in a mood to talk and began to tell her about his wild exploits as a gunslinger. His main trick was to make friends with travelers on the Old Santa Fe Trail, he said, and travel with them a way to discreetly gain their confidence. If he sensed they had money or other valuables, he would murder them in their sleep and steal their money. Another time, he scalped an old man who threatened to hang him for shooting at his cows.

"Sister, now do you think God can forgive me?"

She quoted scripture: "Turn to Me in sorrow of heart and I will forgive, saith the Lord."

"Sister I do not doubt that you believe that God will forgive me: I'm going to tell you what I think God would do. Through you, God is leading me to ask pardon for my many devilish acts. He is enticing me, as I enticed those who had valuables; then when He gets me, He will hurl me into hell, more swiftly than I sent my victims to Eternity. Now what do you think about that, Sister?"

"I will answer you by asking you a question. Who was the sinner who asked Christ to remember him when He came into His kingdom?"

"I don't know, Sister."

"It was the malefactor dying at the side of Christ on the cross who called for mercy at the last moment. He was told by the very Christ-God…thou shalt be with me in Paradise."

She continued to bring him food, clean linens and bandages. She had been doing it for about four months when she came to his door one day to discover he had visitors. One of the ladies present explained their mission: "It was only yesterday that a member of our Methodist congregation was told that the sick man was a Methodist. She went at once to our minister and he appointed this committee, and we are here, ready and willing to attend the sick man."

Sister Blandina replied, "It makes me happy to know the patient will have his own visiting him." She returned to the convent, content that she no longer would need worry about the man. However, two weeks later she was notified that no one had been to see him for a week. That noon, she once again made her way to the sickroom.

When she got there "everything was deathly quiet and the door was ajar. I noiselessly walked in. This is the scene that met me. The patient stretched full length, his eyes glazed and focused on the ceiling, his six-shooter in his right hand with the muzzle pointing to his temple. Quick as a flash I took in the situation and quickly reached the bedside. Placing my hand on the revolver and lowering the trigger while putting the weapon out of his reach."

She said, "The bed is not a good place from which to practice target shooting."

"Just in the nick of time, Sister," he replied. The subject was never mentioned again.

As another month went by, she could tell the patient was visibly losing strength. She contacted his mother, who eventually arrived to take over the chore of nursing her son.

However, she went to visit again and found the man unusually ebullient: "Our patient was quite hilarious. I surmised something unusual had taken place. He lost no time in telling me that 'Billy and the gang are to be here on Saturday at 2 p.m.'" He was anxious to tell her why. "Do you know four physicians who live here in Trinidad? Well, the gang is going to scalp the four of them…because not one of them would extract the bullet from my thigh."

She looked at the sick man for a few seconds then said, "Do you believe that with this knowledge I'm going to keep still?"

"What are you going to do about it?"

"Meet your gang at 2 p.m. next Saturday," she said decisively.

"Saturday, 2 p.m. came and I went to meet Billy and his gang. When I got to the patient's room, the men were around his bed. I can only remember, 'Billy, our captain and Chism.'"

She described Billy: "Steel-blue eyes, peach complexion, is young, one would take him to be seventeen—innocent looking, save for the corners of his eyes, which tell a set purpose, good or bad."

"We are all glad to see you, Sister, and I want to say, it would give me pleasure to be able to do you any favor," Billy said.

She answered, "Yes, there is a favor you can grant me."

He reached out his hand to her, "The favor is granted."

She took his hand, saying, "I understand you have come to scalp our Trinidad physicians, which act I ask you to cancel."

"I granted the favor before I knew what it was, and it stands. Not only that, Sister, but at any time my pals and I can serve you, you will find us ready."

She thanked him and left the room. It would not be long before they would see each other again.

14
The Lamy Murder Trial

The city fathers have caused turnstiles to be put in place of the old gates of the Plaza, which is a vast improvement on their predecessors. They will also be a great aid to those who have been used in the past to do all their love-making with the aid of the stile, and find it hard to reconcile themselves to the primness of parlor spooning.
—*The* Santa Fe New Mexican, *May 10, 1880*

Sister Blandina's next meeting with Billy the Kid, fleeting as it was, was most significant. A leading merchant in Santa Fe, Abraham Staab, asked her in the spring of 1777 if she would accompany his wife and children to Europe. "I believe he thinks money can do anything, and he expects me to accept the offer. When he was convinced that I could not go to Europe, he said he would be satisfied if I would accompany them to the city of New York," she said.

Two weeks later, the archbishop asked her to accompany the Staab family only as far as Trinidad. Sister Blandina stated, "Mrs. Staab, her two children, Sister Augustine and myself, will occupy one carriage; Mr. Staab and two gentlemen who are going to Chicago will ride in another. Everybody is concerned about our going. Mr. Staab spoke to Sister and myself about the danger of travel (at the present time) on the Santa Fe Trail, owing to Billy the Kid's gang. He told us that the gang is attacking every mail coach and private conveyance."

Businessman Abraham Staab. *Courtesy of the Palace of the Governors Photo Archives (NMHM/DCA) negative 011040.*

Staab gave the Sisters a chance to forfeit the trip: "We will have many freight wagons well manned, but if you fear to travel we shall defer the trip."

She asked confidently, "Where could the danger lurk, being in the company of so many freight drivers?" So it was decided, they would make the trip.

In notes to her sister, she revealed the real reason she had no fear: "If ever you get this journal, you will see how very little fear I have of Billy's gang. Even if Billy has mustered new pals, I'm marked for protection as well as anyone wearing my garb."

The trip from Santa Fe to Trinidad was uneventful. But when it was time to make the return trip, the Sisters were again warned of the dangers on the trail. "The Kid is attacking the coaches or anything of profit that comes in his way," they were told. Again, they agreed to make the trip. This time, though, they would not be traveling with a freight wagon train but in a private covered hack, a square-bodied passenger wagon for six people.

The first evening was a stop at the Sweetwater Stage station, halfway between Trinidad and Las Vegas. "It did not take us long to see that extraordinary preparations were being made. The stage driver and his passengers were loading or cleaning revolver and rifles. Ranch men who live in the vicinity showed themselves ready for any emergency."

The Sisters were told, "Billy's gang was dodging around, and we expect they will attack us tonight." The men who were traveling with them said, "Do not be alarmed if you hear firing; we shall protect you."

"Very kind of you, gentlemen, but if you take my advice you will secure a good night's rest and be ready for an early start," Sister Blandina advised.

After breakfast, the Sisters were asked again if it would be wise to continue. "As wise as to remain, we decided. We started. Our span did credit to its trainer, who was driving. About an hour or so after luncheon, the jockey sent his first message of alarm into the carriage," said Sister Blandina.

"Massah, there am som-un skimming over the plains, coming dis way," he yelled in a trembling voice.

"How now, John?" asked Staab.

"Coming fas', massah, right fo' us."

Sister Blandina urged calm: "If the comer is a scout from the gang, our chance is in remaining passive. I would suggest putting revolvers out of sight."

"He am very near," she heard the driver say.

"Please put your revolvers away," she urged the men. The guns went immediately under cover.

She recorded what happened next.

> *The light patter of hoofs could be heard as they drew near the carriage opening. As the rider came from the rear of the vehicle, he first caught sight of the two gentlemen in the front seat, which gave me a chance to look at him before he saw us. I shifted my big bonnet so that when he did look, he could see the Sisters. Our eyes met; he raised his large-brimmed hat with a wave and a bow, looked his recognition, fairly flew a distance of about three rods, and then stopped to give us some of his wonderful antics on bronco maneuvers.*

It was indeed Billy the Kid!

The next day they arrived safely in Santa Fe in record time. "We made the fastest trip every known from Trinidad to Santa Fe."

As the summer of 1880 began to wane and news arrived from Lincoln County in the south where Billy the Kid was still causing much of his havoc, Sister Blandina marveled how a teenage outlaw could be so kind and yet so callous about death. Now, Garrett was charged by U.S. Marshal Sherman to find his old friend, arrest him and bring him to justice.

Now, another event in Santa Fe was daily on Sister Blandina's mind. It was the murder trial of Jean B. Lamy, namesake and nephew of the famous archbishop. The shocking details of the incident were now being revealed at the young man's trial in the city, with Judge L. Bradford Prince presiding. Nearly a year before, young Lamy walked up behind a man at the Exchange Hotel and shot him in the head. Francois Mallet died instantly, shocked bystanders said.

The incident rocked the city and greatly affected the aging archbishop. Recovered somewhat from his illness earlier in the year, now he endured one of the saddest episodes of his life because he loved the murderer and the murdered. The *Santa Fe New Mexican* was giving daily coverage of the aftermath of the shooting, and the Lamy relatives had to suffer through the lurid details.

The archbishop's young nephew arrived in Santa Fe from France ten years before. He was described as an honest, hardworking young man and became known as J.B. Lamy and sometimes as John B. Lamy Jr. to distinguish him from his celebrated uncle. He was not one to carouse or seek societal positions.

Soon, J.B. Lamy met and fell in love with a beautiful young Santa Fe lady, Doña Mercedes Cháves. Daughter of former governor José Cháves, she was a popular socialite in town. She and Lamy soon married and were able to obtain a fine house on lower San Francisco Street. They furnished it with elegant furniture, and Mercedes enjoyed hosting guests at large parties there. The young couple was the toast of the town and became popular houseguests, in no small part because of their famous uncle.

Then late in 1878, Archbishop Lamy sponsored a handsome young architect to travel from France to help with his cathedral project at the top of San Francisco Street. Architect Francois Mallet soon became close friends with the young Lamy couple. When they traveled in their handsome carriage around town, Mallet was often with them. He enjoyed the hospitality of their home.

Soon, rumors were being whispered around that the architect was courting Mercedes Lamy. She became unhappy at home and often quarreled with her husband. Because of her change in attitude, the young Lamy suspicioned that Mallet was the cause. He told him to leave the house and never come again.

In May 1879, Mercedes left home and found lodgings elsewhere. She obtained the services of an attorney and filed for divorce. This, of course, was not sanctioned in the Catholic Church, and the situation became a daily topic for Santa Feans. Mercedes soon was seen strolling in town on the arm of Mallet and was seen being escorted by him to social events.

Her former husband became ill with anxiety over the situation, and he nearly had a nervous breakdown. He hoped for reconciliation with his former wife, but her parading around town with Mallet was more than he could bear. Around September 1, he did the ultimate deed and shot Mallet in the doorway at the Exchange Hotel. He surrendered to two lawmen and was arrested. Mercedes tried to kill herself by drinking poison, but she survived.

As the trial continued during the early days of September, every detail was intently watched and shared by nearly everyone in Santa Fe. A prominent doctor from the Kansas State Medical Association, C.C. Farley, was a witness on the stand, testifying to the mental condition of Lamy. The jury, after a number of attempts to reach a verdict, finally acquitted the murderer by reason of temporary insanity.

"The evidence adduced upon the trial…tended to show that the defendant was insane upon the question of his domestic troubles alone, and at the very sight of the author of his misfortunes, the excitement was so intense that his reason was dethroned and the power to control his actions was destroyed; that his volition was gone, and that he was not morally responsible for his acts," summarized the *Santa Fe New Mexican*. "There was no evidence to show that he was generally insane; but that since the commission of the act his passions had subsided, his excitement was gone and his reason had again assumed its sway. So far as the charge against the defendant is concerned that was disposed of by the verdict of the jury." He was remanded to the city jail and later discharged.

Perhaps due to the Lamy trial, the newspaper focused during this period on gun violence. "The good people of New Mexico are practically unanimous in their condemnation of the dangerous practice of carrying weapons," one article proclaimed. Apparently, another article said the state legislature made carrying guns a crime. But events did not seem to bear that report out.

There was, the newspaper reported, a mysterious disappearance in Santa Fe of a newspaperman from Selma, Kansas. He was boarding at the Grand Central Hotel. It concluded that the case was "suspicious of insanity and suicide." Another man by the name of James Allen was convicted in early August of murder in the first degree in the Santa Fe Court. Train robbers Joseph Stokes and William Mullen were also on trial there. At the same time, the newspaper called the Santa Fe jail "unsafe." In the past six months, several important prisoners escaped, and an armed mob murdered one of the inmates.

But otherwise important progress was heralded on other fronts. The gasworks building was nearing completion, and its crews were expected to install gas lines throughout the city. They expected to begin laying the gas lines earlier than expected, perhaps in September. A study of how to construct dams in the Santa Fe River was proceeding with the goal of installing water lines to city homes. And many new homes were planned in the railroad district as plots were rapidly being sold on the western side of town.

The *Santa Fe New Mexican*, obviously a Republican broadsheet, made much ado about the GOP nomination of Tranquilino Luna to the Forty-Seventh Congress as a New Mexico representative. It emphasized the fact that he was only thirty-one years old and had good pedigree: his grandfather was a captain in the time of the king, his father a man of prominence in the Mexican days and Tranquilino himself was a graduate of St. Louis University. And the city was preparing to fete President Hays and his party who would visit the city in October.

15
Mexico's Hero

The Santa Fe railroad will employ three new Pullman reclining chair cars on night trains, commencing January 1. It is said that these luxuries will be used on the Trinidad branch. It will then be like sailing into heaven in making a trip into New Mexico.
—The *Santa Fe New Mexican, January 3, 1880*

Life in the territory seemed safer now that Apache chief Vitorio was across the border in Mexico. With the new agreement between Mexico and the United States, both armies were now permitted to cross national borders to pursue the renegade chief. In September, his band attacked San Jose, sixty-five miles southwest of El Paso. Twelve Texas Rangers, along with one hundred volunteers were tracking his movements into Mexico and barring him from crossing the border back into Texas.

On the Mexican side, Colonel Joaquín Terrazas, leader of the local militia, was scouring the northern zones of the state of Chihuahua. Terrazas had a force of two hundred that quickly increased to three hundred as volunteers joined his force. He encountered the Americans at the border and politely informed them he would take over the chase. As was their custom to foil their pursuers, Vitorio and his band headed for the safety of the mountains, the Tres Castillos, about sixty miles inside the Mexican border.

Thinking he had lost the Mexican militia, the chief instructed his followers to split up, regroup and meet at a grassy plain beside a lake near three low, rocky peaks of the Tres Castillos. It was an ideal place for the band to rest up, water the horses and feast on cattle they had killed on ranches in the area. They knew the place well and had been there several times before.

With a huge fire roasting the meat, the tribe relaxed as sundown approached. Suddenly rifle fire sounded from all directions around them. Realizing he was surrounded, Vitorio ordered his people to climb the rocky heights of the nearest of the three mountains. They rapidly scaled the heights and hid among the rocks and boulders to wait out the night.

At sunrise, the Mexican soldiers swarmed up the mountainside and hunted down the Indians in their hiding places. The battle raged for two hours, but finally, the Indians' ammunition ran out. At the end of the battle, only sixty-eight women and children were still alive. Reportedly they were sold as slaves in Mexico. Probably the most reliable account about how the chief died was by a warrior who found his body; he said Vitorio stabbed himself with a knife. Colonel Terrazas lost three men.

Terrazas went home to Chihuahua City in triumph. Mexico had a hero! His notoriety and adulations were extra sweet to the citizens of his hometown, who felt he was an even greater hero for having achieved glory without any help from the Americans. They had succeeded whereas the American army had tried to subdue the enemy for over a year.

The real victors in the war against Vitorio, however, were the buffalo soldiers of the 9th and 10th Cavalry. They had multiple skirmishes with the Indians over thousands of blood-stained miles in an unrelenting contest of skill, courage and endurance. Tired, beaten and hounded thousands of miles, the Apaches were losing their will to fight. Vitorio was an easy target for Terrazas, who simply delivered the final blow.

General Pope, still Colonel Hatch's superior, heaped praise on the American soldiers: "It is my duty, as it is my pleasure, to invite the special attention of the authorities to the meritorious and gallant conduct of Colonel Edward Hatch and to Major A. P. Morrow...and the officers and soldiers under their command, in the difficult and trying campaign against the Southern Apaches. Everything that men could do they did, and it is little to say that their services in the field were marked by unusual hardships and difficulties. Their duties were performed with zeal and intelligence and they are worthy of all consideration."

Santa Fe residents seemed unmoved by the dramatic final events taking place in the territory's south and in Old Mexico. Citizens were only affected by those distant events as they watched Army units come and go through the city streets. The soldiers, much adored by locals, were their best source of news from the various war fronts.

Santa Fe 1880

A huge land sale was announced in the city; the *Santa Fe New Mexican* claimed the sale would virtually create a new town near the railyard depot with 224 lots up for grabs. They would line two streets and three avenues. The auction of the lots would add a completely new suburb to the city.

As predicted, by September 22, the long-awaited gas pipelines that would bring lights to the city were being laid, and city residents were excited about Santa Fe becoming the first city in New Mexico to have gaslights in the streets. Fifty men, with sixty burners in hand to weld pipes together, were now engaged in laying those pipes along the main streets.

While Army troops were trying to tame the Wild West, trains from the East continued to disgorge passengers headed to the Southwest in search of new life, hoping that the bustling new cities along the train route would offer new adventure.

One day in late summer, a forty-year-old man of slight build, a compact lean body, slightly thinning hair and a determined look, alighted from the westbound train. He had the face of a scholar. He left the train at the Lamy station and rode by carriage into the city. His mission: discover the ancient culture of the Southwestern Indian tribes to see how they might resemble other primitive people in their evolution toward civilization. He would study their documents and literature and through practical fieldwork trace their social organizations, customs and movements.

Adolph Bandelier was born in 1840 in Bern, Switzerland. His parents migrated to the United States in 1848 and settled in the Swiss immigrant colony of Highland, thirty-five miles east of St. Louis, Missouri. The place was originally named New Switzerland. They became prominent citizens in the town, and when Adolph was in his teens, he returned to Switzerland to study under a leading geologist at Bern University. In January 1861, he returned to Highland and married Josephine Huegy, the daughter of another Swiss immigrant family.

He soon became interested in the pre-Columbian culture of Mexico that he studied from afar, at the Mercantile Library of St. Louis. Then he made contact with the famous American anthropologist Lewis Henry Morgan, who whetted Bandelier's appetite for study of the Southwest Native Americans. He eagerly studied the works of Morgan and another famous explorer of the Southwest, John Wesley Powell. With Morgan as his mentor, Bandelier arrived in Santa Fe sponsored by the Archaeological Institute of America to do fieldwork in New Mexico. He felt especially chosen to receive the contract knowing that some of the institute's directors considered the Indians as "barbarous."

CHRONICLES FROM THE YEAR OF THE RAILROAD

Adolph Bandelier in pueblo ruins, 1880. *Courtesy of the Palace of the Governors Photo Archives (NMHM/DCA) negative 031328.*

The *Santa Fe New Mexican* noted his arrival. It also reported he had a series of meetings with local leaders: Governor Lew Wallace, Archbishop Lamy, territorial librarian/archivist Samuel Ellison and others. Eager to set to work, his first destination was the abandoned Pecos Pueblo Ruins east of Santa Fe, which guarded the southern end of the Rocky Mountains on the Old Santa Fe Trail. At the pueblo ruins, he carefully measured the surviving building walls and counted 517 rooms in the main portion of the pueblo.

"I am dirty, ragged and sunburnt, but of best cheer," he wrote back to Morgan. "My life's work has at last begun." He delighted in the freedom of the open, crisp autumn air of New Mexico.

He did not attempt any excavating at Pecos but he wrote, "The vandalism committed in this venerable relic defies all description…treasure hunters… have recklessly and ruthlessly disturbed the abodes of the dead." He did not attempt to collect any human remains, but he did collect two boxes of artifacts that he sent east to the Harvard University library in Boston. He interviewed several people connected with Pecos and learned that the last inhabitants of the pueblo migrated to the Jemez Pueblo in the mountains east of Santa Fe.

Santa Fe 1880

After his short visit to Pecos, he traveled south on the Camino Real to the Santo Domingo Pueblo, halfway to Albuquerque. The *Santa Fe New Mexican* reported that "Mr. A. Bandolier returned to Cochiti and Santo Domingo yesterday; he is engaged in collecting facts for the American Archaeological Society." Once again, he began measuring buildings and interviewing residents about the history of the community. He asked a photographer, George Bennett, of Santa Fe, to photograph village life. Against tribal leaders' instructions, they intruded on a family burial. This angered the tribe's leaders, and he was asked to leave, having only lived among them for ten days.

He then traveled north a few miles to Cochiti Pueblo, where he was permitted to establish a base. There, no doubt reflecting on his ouster from Santo Domingo, he was on his best behavior, respectful and sensitive to the values of the residents. He again conducted interviews and was allowed to sketch artifacts such as ceremonial objects, arts and crafts. While at Cochiti, he made his first journey into the Jemez Mountains to the sacred valley of Frijoles Canyon. He was enthralled with its majesty and delighted to climb

View of Cochiti Pueblo in 1880, where Bandelier set up his base. *Photograph by John K. Hilliers; courtesy of the Palace of the Governors Photo Archives (NMHM/DCA) negative 002493.*

into the cliff dwellings of the ancient Puebloan peoples. He inspected the ruins of an ancient circular village and marveled at the peace and tranquility of the place as he sat by the flowing stream.

After two months at Cochiti, he traveled back East to regale family and friends with his Southwest exploits and tell of the fabled villages he had visited. But he vowed it would not be the end of his Southwest experience; he planned to return one day to expand his experience among the desert people of the Southwest.

16
A Presidential Visit

Trouble with the Navajos will form part of the headlines of many newspapers for some time if the whiskey selling to these Indians proceeds unchecked as it is now, until the whole thing culminates in an outbreak. Everyone who ought to take this matter in hand is fighting shy of it.
—*The* Santa Fe New Mexican, *December 14, 1880*

Sister Blandina loved Santa Fe. Surrounded by mountains, it reminded her of the Cicagna Mountains of her homeland. Like her childhood home in Italy, she felt totally at home in the old city with its ancient churches and its narrow streets. Her experiences here of several years endeared her to the place. As she walked the streets in the fall of 1880, ambled down the familiar stones of the sidewalks, brushed past the little shops around the plaza, shopped for food at the open market and stuck her head into the mercantile houses downtown, she was wistful. Something in her bones seemed to tell her she might not be staying here much longer.

In late October, she got wind of plans to reorganize the work of the church in the west and in New Mexico in particular. Conferences were being held among the Franciscan order, the Jesuits and the Sisters of Charity. While deliberations continued, she was approached by leaders of the Jesuits, who came to enlist the assistance of the Sisters of Charity to open a school in Albuquerque. Sister Blandina was authorized to negotiate arrangements with the visiting Jesuit leaders. The meeting resulted in an agreement that the Jesuits would build a house, furnished for the Sisters, and donate it to their service. Then they began the planning and collecting of articles that would be of service for the Albuquerque mission.

On a magnificent blue-sky day, she pondered her future as she circled the plaza. The band of the 9th Cavalry was warming up in the center of town. They were about to give one of their weekly concerts. She lingered at a sign that claimed the Swope and Cook Company had eighty-one horses for sale at its stables, "the largest stock of riding and driving animals west of the Mississippi River."

The plaza still had the tattered decorations of the Santa Fe Fiesta some weeks earlier. She remembered the cathedral decorated with lanterns, the streets lighted by bonfires, how she jumped when a canon was fired in the plaza! A High Mass was officiated by Archbishop Lamy. It was a ceremony handed down for three centuries. "Ah, that's my Santa Fe," she must have thought.

She glanced at a sign touting the "finest bath tubs in New Mexico at the O.K. Barber Shop, San Francisco Street." Another announced that Ilfield & Company just received a carload of buggies, ambulances and wagons—all Studebakers from Indiana.

Another sign advertised a play to be performed in Mottley's Theater; *Black Eyed Susan* and *A Serious Family* were on the playbill. A future play would be *Miss Mutton*. She chuckled to herself regarding an incident she heard about at the last performance. A man fell asleep in the darkened theater then, half awake, suddenly started singing "Oh Sing to Me of Jesus." The audience roared with laughter as the man jumped up and made a beeline for the door!

As she headed back home, she probably thought of another story she read in the newspaper that day. "A girl of 13 was to be married to a man in his 30's last night. Friends of the girl's family tried to stop the wedding but legally, anyone over 12 with consent of parents, may marry. A priest was called to do the ceremony—he declared the bride was not over ten years old and he refused to marry a baby! The wedding was called off!" Sister Blandina's chuckle turned into a laugh as she neared the hospital. "What a crazy place," she must have thought, "but I love it!"

The biggest event of the fall season was about to happen: a reception committee for the arrival of President Hayes. Now, the presidential party was expected in a few days, on October 27 or 28. It was reported that General Hatch already left the city for Fort Craig in the west to meet members of the presidential party and escort them to Santa Fe.

In Santa Fe, elaborate plans were being finalized. The planners were at odds about what type of entertainment would be appropriate for the president. He was known as a "temperance man," and some felt a banquet "would be a tame affair without wines, and that it would not be just the thing to invite the president to an entertainment at which they were served," reported the newspaper.

At last, the great day arrived. On October 28, the president's entourage arrived by wagon caravan. State Secretary and acting governor William Ritch, Archbishop Lamy and other dignitaries led the ceremonies on the plaza. The 9th Cavalry Band performed for the president and his wife, Lucy.

Then it was time for the president to respond. "The president said he did not wish to occupy more time," reported the newspaper. "There were several gentlemen among us who were better talkers than he was, and who, he rather suspected, were fond of displaying their talents in that line.

Sketch of President Rutherford B. Hayes. *Clipart courtesy FCIT, https://etc.usf.edu/clipart.*

(Laughter.) Secretary Ramsey was present and he was a very good talker. He was also a good Secretary of War, and he (the president) was convinced that the Secretary was the right man in the right place."

The mayor's wife, Flora Spiegelberg, served as hostess to the president and his wife because they stayed in her home. "As there were no first class hotels in Santa Fe, Lehman Spiegelberg offered the presidential party the hospitality of his home. And there, President and Mrs. Hayes spent the day and evening receiving the officials and citizens of Santa Fe, and a number of the Indian Chiefs."

"It was one of the greatest holidays Santa Fe ever knew," continued Flora Spiegelberg. "And when the President and his wife returned to Washington, they sent us tokens of appreciation…their autographed pictures and invited all of us to visit them, as their guests at the White House, before the end of the administration."

The president and all his entourage seemed to enjoy their short visit. However, one in the party, General William Tecumseh Sherman, general of the U.S. Army and infamous commander of the Union army that sliced through Georgia during the climactic days of the Civil War, had very little that was positive to say about Santa Fe and New Mexico.

The *Santa Fe New Mexican* reported his admonition to local citizens: "You must improve your land, and develop the vast resources of your country, or the new race will come in here and displace you…and get rid of your burros and goats. I hope ten years hence there won't be any adobe houses in the territory. I want to see you learn to make them of brick, with slanting roofs. Yankees don't like flat roofs, nor roofs of dirt." He echoed the sentiments of many people coming from the East.

One of those in the audience that day was the U.S. marshal for New Mexico, John E. Sherman, nephew to the great general. He had been appointed New Mexico's marshal in 1876, probably riding on his high-level connections through the Sherman family of Ohio. He was the son of a well-known attorney and a nephew to Senator John Sherman. He had been in a banking partnership with Frederick Grant, son of President Grant.

Sketch of General William T. Sherman. "I hope ten years hence there won't be any adobe houses in the territory," Sherman said of Santa Fe. *Clipart courtesy FCIT, https://etc.usf.edu/clipart.*

The people of New Mexico were unimpressed with the new marshal's pedigree and welcomed him with little enthusiasm; after all, wasn't his appointment nothing more than political cronyism? In his first four years, he contended with cattle rustlers, stagecoach and highway robberies and a high disregard for the law in all parts of the territory. A major challenge was the sale of spirits to the Indians by unscrupulous liquor runners. Citizen discontent in two counties raged into the Colfax County War and Lincoln County War. Eastern newspapers declared the territory was in the grips of "a virtual reign of terror," and respectable citizens were "paralyzed" in "fear of their lives."

Sherman seemed powerless to tame the wild territory. He only inflamed the strained relationships when he reappointed an impetuous young deputy marshal named Robert Widenmann. His deputy created a storm when he notified the authorities in Washington that the recent murder of cattleman John Tunstall in Lincoln County was engineered by the Santa Fe Ring, that group of lawyers and businessmen who seemed to control most of what was happening in New Mexico. He even claimed the Santa Fe Ring included Lincoln County sheriff William Brady.

Fortunately, Sherman had an ally in territorial chief justice Henry L. Waldo, who felt the vital organs of justice were diseased. The judge was

Santa Fe 1880

Parade scene on San Francisco Street in 1880 led by the buffalo soldiers' marching band.
Photograph by Ben Wittick; courtesy of the Palace of the Governors Photo Archives (NMHM/DCA) negative 087122.

determined to restore law enforcement and the jury system. "There is a total failure in the performance of...duty by those who are required to aid in executing the laws," he said, and "an entire want of efficiency in the administration of justice." He was a good man to have on one's side, Sherman concluded. The judge not only wanted to enforce the laws but he was very gifted in conciliating the quarrelsome political elements of the territory. Even the governor, Lew Wallace, was wary of the political factions at work when he arrived not many months after Sherman. He came to the conclusion that even he was powerless before the informal governmental network of the capitalists and that his office was merely an honor, not a mandate to govern.

Of all the tasks facing the new marshal, the most vexing became the same one that he and the new governor shared as the major challenge of their terms: the Lincoln County War. In the year 1880 that county only had 2,513 inhabitants. But it was the largest county in the west with 20,000 square miles! It had huge waterless plains in the east, rich grazing land in the Pecos Valley and a growing mining industry in its western mountains. Cattle ranches were the main business, with as many as 75,000 head on some of the largest ranches in America.

But the major aspect of life in the county was the mixture of explosive human elements gathered there. In addition to Hispanos, soldiers from the Army that had taken part of the conquest of California made their homes in the region. The lush grasses of the Pecos became home to Texas cattlemen. Anglos were increasingly moving in from the eastern United States. Into this fertile ground came the talented but dangerous acquaintance of Sister Blandina: William H. Bonney, Billy the Kid.

Billy was still causing havoc as a member of the Regulators gang. Not having any luck getting a pardon from Governor Wallace, he went further from the law by continued stagecoach holdups and shootings. By November, the Lincoln County War was heating up again and heading to a climax. The latest news was that Sheriff Pat Garrett vowed to bring the gun-shooter to justice at Santa Fe before the end of the year.

Garrett was raised in Louisiana, one of six children. In 1869, his parents died when he was a gangly six feet four inches tall at age eighteen. He went west to seek his fortune and worked as a cattle driver in the Texas panhandle, then later tried his luck as a buffalo hunter. In 1876, he got into an argument with a mule-skinner by the name of Joseph Briscoe. The argument turned into a fight, and Briscoe came at him with an ax. Garrett pulled his gun and shot the man in the chest; he fell dead at Garrett's feet. It was reported by several men who heard the shot and came running that they found Garrett standing over the dead man, tears running down his ruddy cheeks.

Soon after, Garrett was on a cattle drive to New Mexico when he came into the town of Sumner in Lincoln County. He liked the place and found a job there. After a few months, he decided to go into business for himself and opened a small café in the town. He also became a well-known gambler, and at the tables, he met most of the young men who became some of the most famous gunslingers in the west, including Billy the Kid. The two became close friends, and he became known as "Big Casino" and Billy as "Little Casino" because of their size and because their favorite game was casino poker.

But now, in November 1880, Garrett was the newly elected sheriff, and he became consumed with the goal of capturing the Kid. It was what everyone expected him to do. Not only his honor but also his pride dictated that this was to be his life's greatest moment, when he could ride into Santa Fe with Billy the Kid in custody. Where others had failed, even the governor, he would claim his fame as the one who brought in Billy the Kid.

17
A Tale of the Christ

Young fellows who go about in the wee small hours howling 'in the morning by the bright light' look rather the worse for wear when seen in the morning by the bright light.
—The Santa Fe New Mexican, *December 5, 1880*

For Governor Wallace, the cooler days of November were some of the most blessed days of his life; he expected any day to receive the first copies of the book he had labored over for so many years. As he waited for news from New York of its publication, he remembered when he first conceived of the missive: "In 1875...when I was getting over the restlessness due to years of service in the War of the Rebellion, it occurred to me to write the conceptions which I had long carried in my mind of the Wise Men," of the Christmas story.

"So I wrote, commencing with the meeting in the desert, numbering and naming the three...and ending with the birth of the child in the cave by Bethlehem." Though he had "no convictions about God or Christ. I neither believed nor disbelieved in them...yet when the work was fairly begun, I found myself writing reverentially, and frequently with awe."

He explained that his enthusiasm grew as he wrote by making the book's characters come alive, at least to him. "This is purely natural; for it is with me, presumably, as with every writer who creates as he goes. My characters are essentially living persons. They arise and sit, look, talk, and behave like themselves. In dealing with them I see them; when they speak I hear them. I know them by their features. They answer my call...in turn they call me, and I recognize their voices."

As he wrote about the story he found in the Scriptures, he thrilled at the encounters, the dangers, the glory and the wonder of the story of Christ's birth. Originally, he thought his work would do well as a serial in a magazine. "Well, I finished the proposed serial and deposited it on my desk, waiting for a season of courage in which to open communication with the Harpers," the famous publishing house in New York. "In the time of writing, down to the hour I laid the manuscript by, as said, never once did the possibility of a formal book occur to me." But this end turned out not to be the end.

He wrote:

> *It is possible to fix the hour and place of the first thought of a book...that was a night in 1876. I had been listening to a discussion that involved such elemental points as God, heaven, life hereafter, Jesus Christ and His divinity. Trudging on in the dark, alone except as one's thought may be company good or bad, a sense of the importance of the theme struck me for the first time with force. The manuscript in my desk ended with the birth of Christ; why not make it the first book of a volume, and go on to His death? The story consumed him. I had the opening; it was the birth of Christ. Could anything be more beautiful? As a mere story, the imagination of man has conceived nothing more crowded with poetry, mystery, and incidents pathetic and sublime, nothing sweeter with human interest, nothing so nearly a revelation of God in person. So, too, I saw a fitting conclusion. Viewed purely and professionally as a climax or catastrophe to be written up to, the final scene of the last act of a tragedy or a tale, what could be more stupendous than the Crucifixion?*

With a fierceness of a hunter after his prey, Wallace worked feverishly during his evenings in Santa Fe, desperate to finish the volume. "My custom when night came was to lock the doors and bolt the windows of the office proper, and with a student's lamp, bury myself in the four soundless walls of the forbidding annex. Once there, at my rough pine table, the Count of Monte Cristo in his dungeon of stone was not more lost to the world."

The result: *Ben-Hur: A Tale of the Christ*. And now he was awaiting the first printed copies of his momentous work. Finally, it was released to the public on November 12, for sale at $1.50 per copy. However excited he was to get a copy for himself some days later when it arrived by train in Santa Fe, the

A room in Governor Lew Wallace's abode in the Palace of the Governors was known as the "Ben Hur Room." *Photograph by Christian G. Kaadt; courtesy of the Palace of the Governors Photo Archives (NMHM/DCA) negative 016660.*

news of its debut was not encouraging. Sales were not all that remarkable. Eventually only 2,800 copies were sold in the first seven months. Book critics were not impressed. One wrote in a San Francisco newspaper protesting as a friend of Christ: "He has been crucified enough already without having a Territorial Governor after him!"

Nevertheless, others were congratulatory. Paul Hamilton Hayne, a southern magazine editor, wrote: "I did not think that the man lived in America who could have written such a book...pages in it have thrilled me through and through." Lord Dufferin, former governor of Canada, said, "I sat up the night before last to finish your beautiful book, and I assure you I find it difficult to express my admiration of it." Former president Ulysses S. Grant reportedly could not put it down. He began reading in the morning, he said, finally finishing the book at noon the next day!

Probably the praise most meaningful to Wallace was a letter from future president James Garfield that he kept the rest of his life pressed between pages of one copy of the book. "Dear General," the letter began. "I have this morning finished reading Ben Hur and I must thank you for the pleasure it has given me. The theme was difficult, but you have handled it with great delicacy and power. Several of the scenes—such as the wise men in the desert, the sea fight, the chariot race—will, I am sure, take a permanent and high place in literature. With this beautiful and reverent book you have lightened the burden of my daily life."

Sister Blandina heard another discussion about the book: "Governor Lew Wallace and Mr. Bob Ingersoll were on the train from Santa Fe to Las Vegas. Mr. Ingersoll, looking at the mountains of white clouds and their background of perfect blue, addressed Mr. Wallace in this form: 'Wallace, what is beyond those clouds?...ether? What beyond that...space? And then...I don't know. Do you?' Mr. Wallace made no reply. When his book, Ben Hur, come from the publisher, one copy was forwarded to Mr. Ingersoll with this statement: 'This is the answer to your questions to me on the train from Santa Fe to Las Vegas.' "

Arrival of the published version of the book in Santa Fe not only gave the governor a sense of accomplishment, it also seemed a turning point in his life. He had hints from friends in Washington that he was in for a new assignment, thanks to his support and active campaigning for the newly elected Garfield. He commented, "One is never more on trial than in the moment of excessive good fortune." In the meantime, he had another winter to endure in the high deserts of New Mexico.

The *Santa Fe New Mexican* heralded the new cold season by predicting it would come early this year. Santa Fe citizens shuddered at the news. It was time to get winter clothes out of the storage trunk, for others it was time to air out the buffalo robes, but for all it was time to stack the fire logs. Sister Blandina, no doubt, put the more mobile patients back to work chopping wood for the hospital. The sound of axes chopping wood resounded around the town.

Winter also brought the specter of house fires when cooking mishaps often got out of hand. The good news in the newspaper was that the hook and ladder company was organized to create a volunteer crew ready to deal with any fires. A competitor, the Montezuma Hose Company, was also organized with fifty men committed to fighting for the opportunity to douse the fires.

But the most exciting news in town was about something that would transform life in the old city considerably: the first gaslights were seen in several downtown stores! Santa Fe was the first city in the territory to have gaslights, thanks to work done by the new Santa Fe Gas crews, who had been working for many weeks installing the underground piping. The *Santa Fe New*

Mexican marked December 5 as the first day the lights came on in Santa Fe. Now evening activities would be more enjoyable and safe. The lights would extend people's activities by several more hours a day.

Flora Spiegelberg, who had a gas connection right in front of her house, best captured the novelty of having lights in the city for the first time:

> *It happened just at that time that my husband Willie Spiegelberg was county Commissioner, or Mayor of the city, and in order to confer and honor him, the first gas lamppost was placed in front of our home on Palace Avenue…Like in all small western towns when it was not a bright moonlight night, those that ventured out after dark were obliged to carry lanterns supplied with oil, or a tallow candle…the first gas lamppost created a great sensation in Santa Fe. The old pioneers, Mexicans and Indians, crowded about it staring at the strange bright light and wondering how it came out of an iron pipe! It was most amusing for months nightly to watch the crowds of Mexicans and Indians standing around the lamppost jabbering away, wondering where the light came from.*
>
> *This strange incident occurred the first Saturday night. It was nearly midnight when I was awakened by a Mexican singing loudly, and looking out my bedroom window I saw a man with one hand holding tight to the lamppost, bowing, and swinging his sombrero, saying 'Signora I am delighted to have this great pleasure of dancing a waltz dispassionately with you.' He continued singing and dancing around the lamppost evidently thinking he held the Signora in his arm, and when tired sat down to rest, then began dancing again. Naturally I came to the conclusion that the poor fellow was intoxicated, so I went back to bed. Shortly afterwards I was awakened again by loud pounding on the hall door. My husband was attending a Masonic Lodge meeting, so I was alone with my children and a maid.*
>
> *When the knocking continued, I armed myself and maid with Colt pistols, we walked to the door and from the inside called to the man first in English, then in Spanish to leave immediately or else I would shoot. Repeating my threat a second time then quickly a voice said in Spanish 'My good wife open the door for your husband for he is very sick.'*
>
> *This reply convinced me that the man was no robber, but in his drunken condition had lost his way home. So I asked his name, he answered Juan Lopez, so I said Juan you have made a mistake, this is the house of Don Juan Spiegelberg. I know you live just a block from here so turn around the corner and walk to your home. He mumbled "muchas gracias, Signora," and disappeared!*

Santa Fe 1880

The *Santa Fe New Mexican* declared that the newly illuminated streets would make life easier for law enforcement. It said it would bring to an end "those dangerous and greasy lamps and candles which through three centuries have dimly shown upon the labors of past generations." It was estimated that some 1,200 burners would be necessary to accommodate the demand.

At the same time, Thomas Edison, an electrical engineer, was reporting progress on developing an incandescent lightbulb. His patent 223.898 was granted earlier in the year. A new steamship, the *Columbia*, was the first commercial application of the lightbulb when an electrical system was installed in 1880 in New York City harbor. Edison had confidently said, "We will make electricity so cheap that only the rich will burn candles." It was rumored that Edison expressed interest in New Mexico's booming mining activity in search of high-grade iron ore for his inventions.

As soon as the city had gaslights, another major project was underway: a contract was let for the laying of water lines throughout the city. Instead of running to the river for water, it would spurt from the spigot in every building—indoor plumbing would soon become part of normal life in the territorial capital. And the newspaper announced the establishment of a telephone company, predicting that Bell Telephone phones would be in operation in a few months.

18
Winter Returns

The man who attempted to commit suicide at Carbonetville a few days ago by cutting his throat with a meat knife has sufficiently recovered to be able to walk about the camp. He doesn't like the experiment much and there is not much fear among the miners that he will attempt a repetition of it.
—*The* Santa Fe New Mexican, *page 6, October 24, 1880*

B y Thanksgiving, the city was well into preparations for the holidays when the first snow fell. But with gaslights and indoor plumbing on the way, spirits were bright in a city that started the year in the dark, armed with only the expectations of new beginnings as it joined the rest of the world with improved conveniences and connections. There were still complaints about interruptions of telegraph and mail services, trains oftentimes late on arrival and departure and the challenges of law enforcement. But the progress was palpable, and citizens were still trying to adapt to new realities of life in the capital.

A sign of better things to come was an announcement by the Atchison, Topeka & Santa Fe Railway that it was introducing sleeper cars on the line between Albuquerque and Chicago, "ten feet square and fully ventilated." But incidents along the line continued to be numerous: someone shot at the train fifteen miles south of Albuquerque, and there was a train crash at Raton Pass where eight cars were destroyed. The newspaper accused the railway of causing a freight blockade —it claimed the company was siding freight for Santa Fe in order to rush building materials to the end of the track in southern New Mexico.

Santa Fe 1880

A winter scene at the Santa Fe Plaza. *Photograph by Central Photographic Studio, Erie, Pennsylvania; courtesy of the Palace of the Governors Photo Archives (NMHM/DCA) negative 134572.*

A freight train ran into a passenger train at Galisteo Junction, south of Santa Fe, but caused little damage; passengers were told at 3:00 a.m. that the local train to Santa Fe would not leave until 10:00 a.m. in the morning. Rather than wait seven hours, they decided to walk into town and "arrived at 8, having walked 18 miles in 5 hours!" reported the newspaper.

Nearly every week, the newspaper complained about delays in the U.S. mail service, but there were doubts as to whether it was the train or the mail service that was at fault. It complained of horrible mismanagement of the mail service: "It will pay our people to support the old pony express!" There were other causes: lack of water, snow in Kansas and the telegraph lines were down half the time.

With the arrival of Major John Wesley Powell and a colleague from the Smithsonian Institution, new research was launched to study the habits and customs of the Indians in the Rio Grande Valley. They were planning to visit the Taos, Picuris, San Juan and Santa Clara tribes to gather ethnological and archaeological information. The newspaper wondered if this would be the start of a booming tourist industry.

This was the year of the U.S. Census and enumerator David Catanach counted thirty-eight students at St. Michael's College and fifty students at

View of Santa Fe looking across the river from San Miguel Church on College Street. *Photograph by George C. Bennett; courtesy of the Palace of the Governors Photo Archives (NMHM/DCA) negative 010135.*

the St. Vincent Asylum and Industrial School run by Sister Blandina. Major Powell was apparently given permission to count the Indians for the Census Bureau but "the Indians refuse to answer questions." The paper suggested maybe Indians should be hired to do it. It was Powell's opportunity to officially visit the Pueblo tribes, and it took place the same year as his writing *Introduction to the Study of Indian Languages*.

Notwithstanding the difficulty with mail service, the newspaper continued to share with locals what news came in from around the world, and it ran stories about Sarah Bernhardt, the arrival of the telephone in the West, the Panama Canal scheme and the love letters of Aaron Burr.

Santa Fe 1880

Through the year, the newspaper continued to report on major activities at that burgeoning town just south of the city—Cerrillos. It was the mining center of the territory and caused excitement nationwide, attracting hundreds of aspiring prospectors from the East and their well-heeled sponsors. The newspaper claimed the town now boasted two stores, four saloons, a hotel and a house of ill repute, and another saloon was being built. One mine was bringing up silver, another gold. "The ore shows up well," said the Tennessee and New Mexico Mining Company of their Bonanza II mine.

The man who chronicled the Cerrillos phenomenon best was Santa Fe photographer George Bennett. He spent five days among the miners and left a photographic portfolio depicting the life and trials of miners struggling to find riches in the mountain tunnels. He described the area:

> *The area of the group of mines is 25 or 30 square miles. It is an interesting tract because of ruined and filled up old Indian and Spanish mines, that are being reopened by prospectors and miners that have crowded into the district within a year...there are old mines of "Chalchihuiti" and silver. The former are said to have been worked by Indians before the discovery of America, and the latter were worked under Spanish authority about two hundred years ago. The re-openings disclose old passages, and the ancient tools, potter, and rude implements with which the Aztec, Pueblo, or Spaniard delved for "underground treasure" long ago.*
>
> *"Chalchihuiti," the Indian name for turquoise, is a mineral much prized by the Indians. There is no historical date of commencement to mine for it...though probably it was hunted for upon the surface long before the Spanish conquered and forced the natives to work it out of the rocks for the nobility of Europe to wear. These turquoise mines are said to be the only known ones in America. Some of the most valuable samples now in the crown jewels of Spain, it is said, were taken from these old mines.*
>
> *In 1680 a visitor to Los Cerrillos might have seen drudgery and servitude of mining for poor pay among those who broke the rocks with unwieldy stone hammers, wooden wedges, and levers. In 1880 he can see numerous new mines upon the sites of old ones, and elsewhere hear the pick blows, the scrape and ring of shovelful, the clinking hammer strokes on drills, and the booming of blasts deep in the fissured hills where work in hopeful earnestness is carried on. The prospectors and miners of this district are generally well pleased and reasonably expectant of rich returns for their outlays upon claims, as no silver district heretofore discovered discloses such a great number of true fissure veins in so limited an area of country.*

Turquoise mine near Cerrillos, 1880. *Photograph by Bennett and Brown; courtesy of the Palace of the Governors Photo Archives (NMHM/DCA) negative 014827.*

Bennett's photographs reveal the drudgery and solitude of the miner's life.

One would think Sister Blandina the person least affected by the mining boom, other than the injured miners who frequently came to the hospital for medical assistance. However, on a sunny but cool morning, one of the merchants in town sent Sister Blandina a paper with news from the mining camps. She said, "The headlines gave me a nightmare surprise. In a semi-circle with capital letters was printed: 'Sister Blandina's mine is being worked. Gold found in abundance.'"

She was astounded. "I had heard that some persons in St. Louis were in danger of being financially ruined by bogus advertisements; so when I read this, I took a Sister companion and rode to Los Cerrillos where the supposed mine was located. From some men we had befriended I ascertained who had the untruthful heading printed. I was also told that arrangements had been made to sell stocks of this bogus mine to a certain lady in St. Louis."

In indignation she approached the man: "I understand you are prepared to sell shares on Sister Blandina's mine, which, according to your statement is yielding lode that produces more gold than any mine discovered to date. In a friendly way I advise you to drop your method of getting-rich-quick and resort to hard work instead."

She recognized him from an earlier encounter. In one long breath she said,

> *You remember when you and your so-called company came to me at our hospital in Santa Fe, showing me a specimen of yellow clay claimed by you to have been dug from the southwest corner of our land and which you said had been assayed and showed proximity to a vein of gold and your company corroborated your statement and you asked permission to put your men to work to verify your words? You may also remember my answer: "More to us is the life of the men perishing for want of proper care. If there is gold on our land it can wait a little longer to be discovered." Instinctively I knew you were scheming to deceive, but my intuition did not cover your present line of action. So change your mode of trying to get rich, because it will not work to your benefit either here or hereafter.*

"Do you intend to expose me?" he asked, obviously humiliated.

"You have exposed yourself."

"All right, Sister. You win."

One day in early December, Sister Blandina suddenly sat upright in her chair. In her hand, the *Santa Fe New Mexican* had a startling report from Lincoln County, and it was about her old acquaintance, Billy.

> *The gang of Billy the Kid has been on the warpath: five of them including David Rudebaugh and Billy Wilson started from their den at Portales headed for White Oak, camped at Coyote Springs and were attacked by some White Oak men. They holed up at Koek's Ranch. Jim Carlyle of the White Oak group was invited to a conference and in the afternoon he went to talk to the gang and was detained till nightfall when the gang planned to escape. Carlyle jumped out a window and was shot dead, another miner was killed and another wounded. The gang left for Las Vegas.*

She wondered if he might be heading for Santa Fe.

There was another detailed story in the newspaper that took up two columns of one page. Under a heading called the Crime Calendar, an incident in downtown Santa Fe was reported. The article attempted to demonstrate how far the city had come in its maturity as a law-abiding place.

A party of five men arrived in the city, accompanied by the sheriff of northern Rio Arriba County. They brought with them the story of a shooting affair back in Santa Cruz, a village only a day's ride north of Santa Fe. The article read, in part, as follows:

> *They put up at Herlow's Hotel and on Sunday morning four of them and sheriff Sitnero were arrested on complaint of a Mexican who had just arrived from Santa Cruz with Amado Lucero who was badly wounded in the shoulder. The Mexican alleged that the men had had a hand in the shooting affair at Santa Cruz and so they were all locked up in the Santa Fe jail. From the imprisoned men a reporter of the New Mexican gained the following account of their troubles. On the road just south of Tierra Amerilla they purchased from a small store by the wayside a lot of oat straw that they put upon the wagon after which they proceeded on their way. On Wednesday morning just after they had broken camp they were met by a Mexican who demanded to know where they had gotten the oats that he saw on their wagon.*
>
> *They told him how and where they had secured the provender whereupon he said the oats were his, that they had stolen them and should pay him for them. To this the men replied they had secured the oats honestly and would not pay a cent to him or anybody else. The Mexican then rode off and the men proceeded on their way.*
>
> *The next day the same man, accompanied by another, overtook the party and presented a bill of $75 for the oats and for other alleged depredations committed on property near Tierra Amerilla. The Americans refused to pay*

Santa Fe 1880

the bill, when one of the Mexicans said that they had better settle, as $10 would fix it all right.

The men refused again to pay the bill and the two intruders rode off. Shortly after this, the party was surrounded by a number of men, including Deputy Sheriff Sitnero, and they were arrested.

> They were taken before a Justice of the Peace at Chamita and tried and acquitted. They then went on but were stopped and arrested at Santa Cruz, upon the same charge as before. One of them went back to Chamita and brought deputy sheriff Sitnero to Santa Cruz and he secured their release, by testifying that they had been tried once and acquitted.
>
> While at Santa Cruz on Saturday afternoon a difficulty occurred in a store there between a deputy sheriff named Chas. Krummeek and…Amado Lucero, during which Lucero shot Krummeek, or Dutch Charlie as he was called, and killed him! A deputy sheriff and posse then attempted to arrest Lucero, who ran and was fired at a number of times by members of the posse, one shot taken effect in his shoulder. The men say that they had nothing to do with the shooting and that soon after it occurred they left for Santa Fe with Sitnero, who came with them to ensure them against being further molested.
>
> Very different, however, is the story told by the other side, which is confirmed by several reliable gentlemen who arrived here from Santa Cruz. They say that the party of Americans who had been before the Justice of the Peace for stealing, having been released, endeavored to take the life of the Alcalde and with this object in view they, with Dutch Charlie, went to the house of Amado Lucero where the Justice was and forcing their way in, commenced firing. Lucero defended himself as best he could and finally succeeded in securing his rifle with which he shot Dutch Charlie, who was firing at him as fast as he could. Charlie fell and the men outside commenced firing through the window into the room. Lucero, his wife and the alcalde then ran and managed to escape by another door. Lucero had received a wound in the shoulder…
>
> The above are the two stories of the affair as given by the different sides. Which is true is impossible as yet to ascertain, but as Lucero bears a good character many persons who know him are rather disposed to believe his account. The men who are under arrest…are endeavoring to secure bail. Dutch Charlie, the dead man, was a notoriously hard character and his taking off is not very deeply regretted.

On Sunday a good deal of excitement was created in this city by the rumor that the Mexicans had threatened to avenge Lucero's wrongs by taking the prisoners from jail and lynching them. All day this was the topic of conversation and the public was forcibly reminded of the day that preceded the brutal murder of James Donigan at the hands of a...mob. The people who talked the matter over did not know the merit of the case, or whether the men in jail were or were not guilty, and they did not care to know when the question of lynching was under consideration.

Several men took it upon themselves to call upon sheriff Jose D. Sena for the purpose of acquainting him with the state of affairs...reporting that he was not at home. Then the citizens began to take the matter into their own hands and before dark probably a hundred and fifty men had volunteered to guard the jail through the night. Every man was quiet and determined, bent on preventing mischief and not on creating it.

In fact it was simply a strong expression of the public sentiment on the lynching question and an expression that peremptorily declares that no such brutal outrages as that which a few months ago disgraced Santa Fe shall occur. From nine o'clock till day break the jail was guarded by a large body of men and about 12 o'clock, at the instance of acting Governor Ritch, Sheriff Sena went down and swore in ten deputy sheriffs from the crowd and appointed a large posse to watch till morning.

In the face of this demonstration, of course, no attempt on the jail was made and the night passed away without bloodshed of any kind. This affair, however, will have a wholesome effect as it made it very plain that Judge Lynch will not be countenanced in Santa Fe and that it will not be very healthy for those who undertake to administer lynch law again.

19
The Kid Comes Back to Santa Fe

Governor Lew Wallace has issued a proclamation offering a $500 reward for the capture and delivery to the Sheriff of Lincoln County of William Bonney, alias "The Kid." This is a good step and will make it too hot in New Mexico for the prominent young man who is so much desired by the executive.
—*The* Santa Fe New Mexican, *December 14, 1880*

Among all of the accusations against Billy the Kid, a new one was lodged in late autumn: counterfeiting. Treasury Secret Service agent Azariah F. Wild arrived in Lincoln County to collect evidence against Tom Cooper and William Wilson, supposed associates of Billy the Kid. When he felt he had enough evidence to present a case against them, he asked Marshal Sherman for help in bringing the men in. After a first refusal by the marshal, Wild then found some men in Sumner who claimed they were willing to form a posse to do the job. With this news, Sherman agreed to deputize them.

Of those deputized, Sheriff Pat Garrett soon took charge of the posse. One of his sidekicks, Robert Olinger, joined the group. Cattle detective Charles Siringo and Frank Stewart, of the Canadian River Cattlemen's Association, also assisted Garrett. Sherman readily issued federal murder warrants for the perpetrators of the Lincoln County War, including Billy the Kid.

On the evening of December 19, the posse ambushed the Kid's band at an abandoned building in Fort Sumner. They killed one member,

The only known studio portrait of William H. Bonney, "Billy the Kid." *Courtesy of the Palace of the Governors Photo Archives (NMHM/DCA) negative 030769.*

Tom O'Folliard, but the others got away. It was reported that O'Folliard hysterically cried, "Don't shoot any more, for God's sake. I'm already killed." One in the posse said, "Take your medicine." Apparently O'Folliard lived a few hours more and by one account said, "Garrett, I hope to meet you in hell." To which Garrett replied, "I would not talk that way, Tom. You are going to die in a few minutes." As he lay dying, the men sat around him playing a game of cards.

The next day at about noon, a rancher came to them; "Boys, the Kid and his bunch had supper at my house and have gone over to that rock house on the Taiban." They saddled up and headed for Taiban Creek. As they were closing in on the Kid, Garrett suddenly realized that the commissions of his posse given by Sherman would expire on January 1, 1881. Fearing their commissions would expire before they captured the Kid, he sent two of his men to Santa Fe to have the commissions extended by Sherman, only to hear that the marshal was in Washington, D.C.

Garrett's concern about the commissions turned out to be the least of his worries because on December 23 the posse came upon Billy's gang at Stinking Springs in the cattle country of Lincoln County, about fifteen miles east of Fort Sumner. They came to a one-room house next to an arroyo that had only one door and a little window. They saw the outlaws' horses tied up to the *vegas*, roof poles of the little shack. They figured out that there were four men in the house with Billy—Charlie Bowdre, Dave Rudabaugh, Tom Pickett and Billy Wilson, the Kid's closest friends and most ardent followers.

Pat Garrett (1850–1908), the sheriff who brought Billy the Kid to Santa Fe in December 1880. *Photograph by James N. Furlong; courtesy of the Palace of the Governors Photo Archives (NMHM/DCA) negative 105080.*

It was two days before Christmas and the snow was deep; the men cautiously surrounded the house. As nightfall came, the hidden men kept a close eye as temperatures began to drop below freezing. The lanky Garrett stepped out from cover in the moonlight and called for the gang to surrender.

The Kid's response was typical; he fired shots in the direction of the sound of his former friend's voice. Garrett's men, about twenty strong, opened a volley of fire on the house. When Bowdrie crossed in front of the window, he was hit in the chest by a bullet and let out a piercing scream, "I'm killed, Billy, they killed me!"

By one account, Billy shoved him to the door and told him, "They have murdered you, Charlie, but you can get revenge, go out there and kill them before you go!" He shoved his friend out the door into a hail of bullets. Bowdrie lifted his six-shooter but did not have the strength to pull the trigger. He staggered forward blindly until he fell into Garrett's arms. The lawman put him into his own bedroll, where his last words were "I wish—I wish—I wish."

Gunfire was exchanged periodically between the two sides for two days. At one point Garrett shouted: "How are you doing, Kid?"

Charles Bowdre, killed at the Taiban by Pat Garrett's posse, and his wife, Manuela Herrera Bowdre, 1878. *Photograph by James N. Furlong; courtesy of the Palace of the Governors Photo Archives (NMHM/DCA) negative 105048.*

Santa Fe 1880

"Pretty well, but we have no wood to get breakfast."

Garrett responded, "Come out and get some. Be a little sociable." He then ordered his men to build a fire and fry up some bacon and eggs so the aroma would waft toward the house.

On the second day, a white handkerchief suddenly appeared at the top of the chimney, tied to a Winchester barrel. Garrett asked them what they wanted, and Billy said they wanted to surrender on condition that they would be given safe passage to Santa Fe. Garrett agreed to the condition, and the four men stumbled out of the house, starving and panting for water.

The posse and the prisoners spent the night at a nearby ranch. The next day, Christmas Eve, they headed for Fort Sumner, where the prisoners were put in shackles. They traveled all Christmas Day and arrived in Las Vegas that night, where they were met by crowds of curious onlookers. A reporter for the *Las Vegas Gazette* interviewed the Kid that night. He noted he seemed very relaxed. Billy replied, "What's the use of looking on the gloomy side of everything? The laugh's on me this time."

The next day as the prisoners were loaded onto the Santa Fe westbound train, they were surrounded by an armed mob. But Billy was not the object of their anger. Local Deputy Sheriff Romero, backed by an angry group of men, demanded custody of Dave Rudabaugh for his murder in 1879 of Las Vegas deputy sheriff Lino Valdez.

Garrett refused to hand over the prisoner and, according to a report in the *Santa Fe New Mexican*, said, "If you want him, you've got to take him." Disaster was averted when Garrett agreed to permit the local sheriff and a deputy ride on the train with them to Santa Fe where they could request Rudabaugh's return to Las Vegas. When they arrived in Santa Fe a few hours later, the *Santa Fe New Mexican* reported members of the posse said, "The demonstration at Las Vegas was of a serious nature and not to the credit of the town." The editor declared, "Sheriff Pat Garrett gave New Mexico quite a Christmas gift!"

Reporting further, the newspaper account read:

> *The Kid, Wilson and Rudabaugh were jailed in Santa Fe at about 7:30 Monday evening. Tuesday morning at 11 o'clock when Pat Garrett and his men went down to see them, it was discovered that they had had not a mouthful to eat since they were put in jail. Upon which one of the posse when down to the keeper of the restaurant who had a contract for feeding United States prisoners and asked him why he had not sent down meals to the three. The man said he had done so, and after a little investigation*

it was discovered that Jailer Silva or some of his henchmen had eaten the grub themselves. It's pretty rough on prisoners when their jailers eat the meals sent to them.

In jail, Billy revived his campaign to obtain a pardon from Governor Wallace. No doubt he asked to go to the governor as soon as he arrived in the capital. During his time in that prison, he sent four letters to the governor asking for an audience so that he could explain why he deserved a pardon. Wallace refused to intervene.

The young outlaw became the center of attention. Marshal Sherman enjoyed taking wide-eyed spectators to the jail where they would stand speechless and gape at the prisoner. The Kid finally complained to the governor, "I am not treated right by Sherman. He lets every stranger…see me through curiosity…but will not let a single one of my friends in." The Kid was so distraught that he and Rudabaugh attempted to dig their way to freedom. Had not Chief Deputy Marshal Tony Neis and Sheriff Romulo Martinez caught them in the act, they would have escaped!

But eventually one of those visitors who would venture in to see him was a friend, and one might say, the best friend Billy the Kid ever had—Sister Blandina. She left a vivid description of her visit:

> *The two prisoners were chained hands and feet, but the Kid besides being cuffed hands and feet was also fastened to the floor. You can imagine the extreme discomfort of the position.*
>
> *When I got into the prison-cell and Billy saw me, he said—as though we had met yesterday instead of four years ago—"I wish I could place a chair for you Sister." At a glance I saw the contents of the prison. Two empty nail kegs, one empty soapbox, one backless chair…after a few minutes' talk, the Kid said to me, "Do what you can for Kelly…This is his first offense, and he was not himself when he did it." Then he assured her of his own situation, "I'll get out of this; you will see, Sister."*

"Think, dear Sister Justina," she mused to her sister, "how many crimes might have been prevented, had someone had influence over Billy after his first murder. The plains are broad. His ascendancy was instantaneous over the minds of our free-lance cowboys, who are spurred on by a freedom that is not freedom. Finding himself captain and dictator, with no religious principles to check him, he became what he is—the greatest murderer in the Southwest. I marvel at the assurance of the chained youth. No one can surmise how he can escape punishment this time. Mr. Kelly, his companion prisoner, is much dejected—fully realizing the enormity of his crime."

The *Santa Fe New Mexican* carried an interesting story in its December 29 edition: "Acting Governor Ritch has just received a letter from Lincoln County, written for Charles Bowdre, the outlaw who was killed at Stinking Springs by Sheriff Pat Garrett's posse...in which Charlie's surrender is proposed upon the condition that the indictments against him for the murder of Roberts in the Lincoln County War and his other offenses be abolished. It is not very probable that the authorities would have complied with any such conditions, but however this may be, Charlie is now where no indictments will reach him."

As the old year waned and snow fell on the city, from the governor's office to the Sister's hospital, from the still-rising walls of the cathedral to the new mansions on Palace Avenue, there were sighs of relief as people in the capital enjoyed the quietest New Year's night in many years.

20
Varied Destinies

A man who spoils a sensation by deliberately telling the truth to a reporter,
is fit for treason or the Senate. This paragraph is all that remains
of a two column article.
—*The* Santa Fe New Mexican, *March 3, 1880*

Archbishop Lamy, having endured many long journeys in the Southwest desert as well as trips across the Atlantic, continued to serve as head of the territorial church until 1885, when he resigned and was appointed titular archbishop of Cyzicus, a distant place in a world far away that was overrun by infidels long years before. But he lived long enough to see his beloved Cathedral Basilica of St. Francis of Assisi in Santa Fe dedicated in 1887.

A year later, at age 74, he again fell ill, contracted pneumonia and passed away, no doubt in the arms of his beloved niece Maria. He was laid to rest under the floor of his enduring monument at the end of San Francisco Street, the Basilica Cathedral of St. Francis of Assisi. The small village of Galisteo Junction, where trains stop for Santa Fe passengers, was renamed Lamy in his honor. It is not far from the quarry where the sandstone blocks for the walls of the cathedral were carved from the earth. Today, a bronze statue stands in his memory in front of the basilica.

There was a somewhat happy ending for young Jean-Baptiste Lamy, the archbishop's nephew, and Mercedes: they eventually reconciled and spent married life together for many years afterward.

SANTA FE 1880

Archbishop Jean-Baptiste Lamy lying in state in Loretto Chapel, 1888. *Photograph by Brother Amian; courtesy of the Palace of the Governors Photo Archives (NMHM/DCA) negative 055185.*

Governor Lew Wallace resigned from his duties as territorial governor on March 9, 1881, and soon after returned to his hometown of Crawfordsville, Indiana, to await a new political appointment. The wait was not long. On May 19, he was appointed U.S. minister to the Ottoman Empire in Constantinople, where he remained until 1885. While there, he became a trusted friend of the sultan, Abdul Hamid II. One of his joys was to visit Middle Eastern locations where he imagined his Ben-Hur might have traveled.

He continued to write after his return from Turkey, but his greatest satisfaction came from planning a monumental private study at his home in Crawfordsville. It was there that he died on February 15, 1905, from atrophic gastritis at age 77. He was buried in the town's Oak Hill Cemetery. The State of Indiana commissioned sculptor Andrew O'Connor to create a marble statue of him, dressed in a military uniform, to be placed in the U.S. Capitol in Washington, D.C. A bronze copy of the statue stands on the grounds of his Crawfordsville study.

William Bonney, "Billy The Kid," languished in the Santa Fe jail through March 1881, when he was then sent south to be tried for murder. Convicted, he was sent back to the Lincoln County jail to wait his hanging day. While there, he fooled the jailkeeper by insisting that he needed to go out to the latrine. Once out of his cell, he grabbed the man's gun and shot him dead. Another deputy came running from across the street, and Billy shot him dead as well. Billy the Kid was on the loose again!

Almost three months after his escape, Sheriff Garrett responded to rumors that Bonney was in the vicinity of Fort Sumner, and he began a new search for the Kid. Accompanied by two deputies, he headed for the home of Pete Maxwell, known to be a friend of Bonney's. Maxwell and Garrett chatted for a while and around midnight while they sat in Maxwell's darkened room, Billy entered. Not recognizing the sheriff, Billy asked *"Quien es? Quien es?"* Those turned out to be his last words in life. Garrett drew his revolver and shot two times. The first bullet reportedly hit Bonney in the chest, just above his heart. One of America's most famous Wild West characters was dead. Newspapers claimed he killed one person for every year that he lived—he died at age twenty-one.

Garrett was anxious to collect his reward from the governor, so five days after the killing, he traveled to Santa Fe. By the time he arrived, Wallace was gone and acting governor William Ritch was seated in the governor's chair. He refused to pay the reward, but over the next few weeks, residents from around the territory raised over $7,000 as a reward for Garrett. A year later, the New Mexico Legislature passed a special act to provide the $500 bounty that Governor Wallace had promised.

Garrett became famous as Bonney's killer but the manner that he had done it brought severe criticism. To people who idolized the young desperado, the Kid was the victim of a traitorous friend. At the end of his term as sheriff, the Republican Party refused to back Garrett, and he went into ranching.

Santa Fe 1880

The Maxwell House in Fort Sumner where Billy the Kid was shot by Pat Garrett. *Courtesy of Palace of the Governors Photo Archives (NMHM/DCA) negative 045559.*

After some years in that business, he met a tragic shooting death in 1908, at age fifty-eight, while in the company of a business partner who claimed he shot him in self-defense during an argument.

General Edward Hatch, who spent most of his time in the west chasing Indians, would live to see a temporary cessation of hostilities in New Mexico, but the Indian Wars in the West would not finally end for six more years. He died on April 11, 1889, at age fifty-six and was buried in the Fort Leavenworth National Cemetery in Kansas.

The work of the buffalo soldiers continued for a number of years around the Southwest. Mostly, they were called time and again to battle the restless Indians when they broke out from their U.S. government-appointed reservation confines. The skirmishes would continue until the last chieftain made peace; Geronimo surrendered to the U.S. Army in 1886.

Adolph Bandelier returned to New Mexico in 1882 and continued research at the pueblos of Cochiti, Acoma and Tesuque, but his wife's poor health caused the couple to return to their hometown in Highland. After a few months there, he returned to visit the Laguna, Acoma and Zuni Pueblos. In 1884, the family bank in Highland failed, and he was accused of being

Outlaw Billy the Kid's tombstone at Fort Sumner, Lincoln County. His friend Charlie Bowdre is buried next to him. *Photograph by Barns & Caplin; courtesy of the Palace of the Governors Photo Archives (NMHM/DCA) negative HP.2007.20.112.*

partly the cause for its demise. In late 1885, he returned with his wife to Santa Fe for five more years.

In 1913, the couple sailed for Spain to do research at the Seville historical archives. Six months later, his health quickly deteriorated, and he died on March 18, 1914. His wife stayed on in Spain another year and a half to continue the research he started. His mortal remains were exhumed in Seville in 1977 and sent to New Mexico. There he was cremated, and his ashes were scattered in Frijoles Canyon in Bandelier National Monument, near Los Alamos.

Doc Holliday parted ways with Wyatt Earp in 1882 when Earp decided to pack off with his family to California. Holliday decided he preferred the dusty Southwest towns where he felt most comfortable. Part of the dwindling cadre of Wild West gunmen, he preferred to stick to the backwater towns of the West. His tuberculosis progressed so that often he would cough for several days. His luck at the card tables was also waning until by 1887 he was a destitute, emaciated wreck. He decided to go to his favorite health spa in Glenwood Springs, Colorado, to get relief for his ailments and died in his bed on November 8, 1887, at age thirty-six. It is said he died with a shotgun, a Bowie knife and his nickel-plated six-shooter next to him.

As for Sister Blandina, after four years in Santa Fe, she went to Albuquerque where, besides her work of teaching, she opened a Wayfarers' House, became a defender of Native Americans and "Mexicans" and went on fundraising trips to mining and railroad camps to support the Sisters' missions. Later, she returned to Trinidad and also spent a short time in Pueblo, Colorado.

She traveled to Ohio in 1893 and four years later was sent with her sister Justina to see if they could do anything for the poor Italian immigrants in the inner city of Cincinnati. Going to explore the conditions with only five dollars in their pockets, these two sisters founded and managed Santa Maria Institute, the first Catholic settlement house in the United States, in 1897. They enlisted assistance from numerous sources and established services of every description to help the poor and needy. In the process, they visited the jails and charity wards in the hospitals and became involved in issues such as human trafficking and juvenile delinquency.

In 1900, Sister Blandina returned to Albuquerque for two years to help start St. Joseph Hospital, known as CHI St. Joseph's Children Health, where poor children received early-childhood services. In 1933, at the age of eighty-three, Sister Blandina retired to the Sisters of Charity motherhouse in Cincinnati. There, she prayed and maintained a lively correspondence with her many friends and acquaintances.

To the Sisters who came into her room in the infirmary, she would say, "Child pray that God may give me the grade to endure, to persevere." When terrific headaches would strike her, she would smile and say, "From my mother I have inherited these bad headaches. My mother's name was Malatesta, which means "bad head." And all my life I have had this 'bad head.'"

"How do you feel this morning, Sister?" the Sisters would ask her.

"Just as God wills," she always replied.

In response to "What can I do for you, Sister?" she would answer, "No, child, not for me, but for God." Then she would say, "He must be very pleased with you, child. Always keep your chin up, and your eyes on God."

The end came on February 23, 1941, just a month after the celebration of her ninety-first birthday. Sister Therese Martin described her final days:

Her Sisters in Christ and her friends watched and prayed. And throughout the city news spread that Sister Blandina was dying. The Italians of Cincinnati were grief stricken. Had she not instructed 80 per cent of them herself?

But Sister Blandina was worrying about neither past nor future. She was a little girl again in Cincinnati, sitting in a fruit wagon and looking into the faces of the first two Sisters of Charity she had ever seen. And then she was turning to Il Signorino, her father and saying to him, "Father, as soon as I am old enough I shall be a Sister of Charity."

And she had been a Sister of Charity in the fullest sense for over seventy years. Her last aspiration was, "My Jesus, Mercy…Gesu…Madre." The sun came out just as the priest blessed the grave, and her many friends were reminded of her brilliant smile that had blessed so many of them.

She was buried in the motherhouse graveyard, next to her sister Justina, who died several years before.

Selected Bibliography

Anderson, George B., ed. *History of New Mexico, Its Resources and People, Vol. 1*. Los Angeles: Pacific States Publishing Company, 1907.
Ball, Larry D. *The United States Marshals of New Mexico and Arizona Territories, 1846–1912*. Albuquerque: New Mexico University Press, 1978.
Boomhower, Ray E. *The Sword and the Pen, A Life of Lew Wallace*. Indianapolis: Indiana Historical Society Press, 2011.
Bryant, Keith L., Jr. *History of the Atchison, Topeka and Santa Fe Railway*. Lincoln: University of Nebraska Press, 1974.
Chamberlain, Kathleen P. *Victorio*. Norman: University of Oklahoma Press, 2006.
Chávez, Thomas E. *An Illustrated History of New Mexico*. Albuquerque: University of New Mexico Press, 2003.
———. *New Mexico Past and Future*. Albuquerque: University of New Mexico Press, 2006.
Cline, Donald. *Alias Billy the Kid, The Man Behind the Legend*. Santa Fe, NM: Sunstone Press, 1986.
Fialka, John J. *Sisters: Catholic Nuns and the Making of America*. London: Macmillan, 2004.
Fried, Stephen. *Appetite for America*. New York: Bantam Books, 2010.
Frost, Richard H. *The Railroad and the Pueblo Indians*. Salt Lake City: University of Utah Press, 2016.

Selected Bibliography

Garrett, Pat F. *The Authentic Life of Billy the Kid*. Santa Fe: New Mexico Printing and Publishing Company, 1882.

Horgan, Paul. *Great River, The Rio Grande in North American History*. Middletown, CT: Wesleyan University Press, 1984.

———. *Lamy of Santa Fe*. New York: Ferrar, Strauss and Giroux, 1975.

Kenner, Charles L. *Buffalo Soldiers and Officers of the Ninth Cavalry 1867–1898, Black and White Together*. Norman: University of Oklahoma Press, 1999.

Leckie, William H. *The Buffalo Soldiers*. Norman: University of Oklahoma Press, 1967.

Marshal, James. *Santa Fe: The Railroad that Built an Empire*. New York: Random House, 1945.

McGoffin, Susan Shelby. *Down the Santa Fe Trail and into Mexico*. New Haven, CT: Yale University Press, 1926.

Nash, Jay Robert. *Encyclopedia of Western Lawmen & Outlaws*. New York: Paragon House, 1992.

Niederman, Sharon. *A Quilt of Words, Women's Diaries, Letters & Original Accounts of Life in the Southwest, 1860–1960*. Boulder, CO: Johnson Publishing Company, 1988.

Pacheco, Ana. *A History of Spirituality in Santa Fe*. Charleston, SC: The History Press, 2016.

Prince, L. Bradford. *A Concise History of New Mexico*. Cedar Rapids, IA: The Torch Press, 1914.

Roberts, David. *The Pueblo Revolt, The Secret Rebellion that Drove the Spaniards Out of the Southwest*. New York: Simon & Schuster, 2004.

Ruxton, George F. *Adventures in Mexico and the Rocky Mountains*. London: John Murray, 1847.

Santa Fe New Mexican. December issues in 1879 and all issues for year 1880.

Schroeder, Albert, ed. *The Wonderful Year of 1880*. Santa Fe, NM: La Gaceta, El Corral de Santa Fe Westerners, Vol. V, No. 3, 1971.

Segale, Sister Blandina. *At The End of the Santa Fe Trail*. Milwaukee: Bruce Publishing Company, 1948.

Simmons, Marc. *Yesterday in Santa Fe*. Santa Fe, NM: Sunstone Press, 1989.

Tobias, Henry J. and Charles E. Woodhouse. *Santa Fe, A Modern History, 1880–1990*. Albuquerque: University of New Mexico Press, 2001.

Wallace, Lew. *Lew Wallace, An Autobiography*. New York: Harper & Brothers, 1906.

Wallace, Susan E. *The Land of the Pueblos*. New York: John B. Alden, Publisher, 1888.

Selected Bibliography

Weigle, Marta, ed. *Telling New Mexico: A New History*. Santa Fe: Museum of New Mexico Press, 2009.

Wilson, Chris. *The Myth of Santa Fe, Creating a Modern Regional Tradition*. Albuquerque: University of New Mexico Press, 1997.

About the Author

Dr. Allen R. Steele spent his life in communication media, first as a disc jockey at his college radio station, then moving up to managerial and administrative positions in international broadcasting networks. He also spent many years as a university professor in Australia and America. More recently, he has immersed himself in the history of the Southwest. Among his previous books, *The French Pilot* gained widespread respect for its portrayal of a French Huguenot ship's captain who braved the religious turmoil of France and eventually migrated to New York. He now resides in Santa Fe and enjoys sharing the city's history with visitors on his downtown history tours.

Visit us at
www.historypress.com

www.ingramcontent.com/pod-product-compliance
Lightning Source LLC
Chambersburg PA
CBHW042140160426
43201CB00021B/2351